The Church Treasurer's Manual

The Church Treasurer's Manual

A Practical Guide for Managing Church Finances

Bruce Nuffer, editor

BEACON HILL PRESS
OF KANSAS CITY

Copyright 2003, 2008
by Beacon Hill Press of Kansas City
First edition 2003
Second edition 2008, with title change

ISBN: 978-0-8341-2383-0

Printed in the
United States of America

Cover Design by Arthur Cherry
Interior Design by Sharon Page

Permission is granted upon purchase to adapt and print many of the forms contained on the CD. See readme file on CD for details. All permissions granted for noncommercial use within the local church.

Disclaimer: *The Church Treasurer's Manual* contains general information. It does not offer specific legal or tax advice. Such advice and answers to technical accounting questions should be secured from legal counsel or qualified accounting professionals.

The editor and Beacon Hill Press of Kansas City disclaim any liability, loss, or risk—personal or otherwise—incurred as a consequence, directly or indirectly, of the use or application of any contents of this work.

Library of Congress Cataloging-in-Publication Data

Nuffer, Bruce, 1967-
　　The church treasurer's manual : a practical guide for managing church finances / Bruce Nuffer, editor. — 2nd ed.
　　　p. cm.
　　Rev. ed. of: The church treasurer's handbook.
　　Includes bibliographical references.
　　ISBN 978-0-8341-2383-0 (pbk., with accompanying compact disc of resources) 1. Church finance—Handbooks, manuals, etc. I. Nuffer, Bruce, 1967- Church treasurer's handbook. II. Title.

　　BV770.N84 2008
　　254'.8—dc22

　　　　　　　　　　　　　　　　　　　　　　　　　　　　　　　　　　　　2008019981

DEDICATION

To my dad, who I envision is what every church treasurer ought to aspire to be.

ACKNOWLEDGMENTS

Special thanks to Warren Nuffer, Kevin Brown, Barry Russell, and Gabriele Steinhart. And special thanks also to Don Walter and the Church of the Nazarene Pensions and Benefits office; Esther Diley and the Evangelical Lutheran Church of America; Art Rhodes and the Church of God (Anderson, Indiana); Steve Dennie and the Church of the United Brethren in Christ, USA; and Dan Busby, acting president of the Evangelical Council for Financial Accountability, Washington, D.C.

EDITOR'S NOTE TO THE READER

The Church Treasurer's Manual is designed to place at fingertips a number of resources to assist the treasurer in the fulfillment of this vital church ministry. In researching and compiling the content of this book, the editor requested permission to use substantive material from sources listed in "Works Cited." In the interest of developing continuity and seamless flow, the editor included transitions and weaved his words with the language from these sources. Attention has been given to distinguishing the material where possible. Where the editor's writing and the content from other sources are blended, the editor gratefully acknowledges his appreciation to the providers of information that is specific and technical to the needs of church treasurers.

CONTENTS

Introduction	11
1 Responsibilities of the Church Treasurer	15
Separation of Financial Responsibilities	16
Guidelines for Handling Church Offerings	17
Acknowledging and Reporting Charitable Gifts	22
Quid Pro Quo Disclosure Requirements	32
Suggested Steps in Handling Expenditures	37
Should You Computerize Your Church's Financial Records?	39
2 Payroll, Employees, and Ministerial Compensation	41
Who Is an Employee, and Who Is a Contractor?	41
Employees	42
Contractors, Employees, and Ministers	51
Employees (Other than Clergy)	52
Clergy	52
What If We Do Not Withhold and Report?	54
What If We Are Not Sure Which Employment Relationship Exists?	55
10 Steps to Preparing for Payroll Tax Obligations	55
Ministerial Compensation	60
IRS Regulations for Business Expense Reimbursements	62
The Cost of a Minister vs. the Cost of a Ministry	63
Parsonage or Housing Allowance?	66
Pro Parsonage and Con Housing Allowance	67
Pro Housing Allowance and Con Parsonage	68
Tax Implications	69
Another Alternative	70
OK. We've Decided on the Housing Allowance	71
Conflict over Compensation Issues	77
3 Taxes	79
Tax and Reporting Procedures for Congregations	80
Classification of Employees	80
How the Courts Have Ruled	81
The Ministerial Employee	82
The Lay Employee	83
The Employer Identification Number	83

What Is Taxable for Federal Income Tax Purposes?	84
Income Tax Withholding	86
Social Security/Medicare Tax Witholding	86
Form W-4	87
Deposit of Withheld Amounts	88
Form 941	88
Form W-2	90
Form W-3	93
Form W-5	94
Form 1099-MISC	94
Records	94
Short Checklist for Tax Procedures	94
Checklist for Filling Out Box 1 of Form W-2	95
Minimizing Income Taxes for Church Employees	96
Tax-Free Employee Benefits	97
Business Transportation, Travel, and Related Expenses	97
The Accountable Reimbursement Plan	100
What the Church Could Do	101
The Church-Owned Automobile	103
Summary	105

4 Budgeting, Reporting, and Financial Audits — 107

How Do You Determine the Annual Budget?	107
The Chart of Annual Accounts	110
Financial Reports to the Congregation	112
Balance Sheet	113
Statement of Revenue and Expense	113
Statement of Cash Flows	113
Other Financial Reports	113
Audits	114
Why Have an Audit?	114
External Audits	115
Internal Audits	115
Audit Procedures	116

Works Cited — 123

Appendix 1 Where to Go for More Information — 125

Appendix 2 Financial Forms — 127

INTRODUCTION

THEFT TESTS SMALL CHURCH

Kansas City: The announcement came after the sermon, after the singing of the hymns, after the passing of the collection plate.

Thomas E. Sims—a member of the First Presbyterian Church of North Kansas City for 33 years—stepped up to the pulpit with some grim news.

He was tight-lipped, his face drawn. He slipped on his reading glasses and began telling members about one of their own.

Kent Issac Skidmore, 48—who grew up in the church, who most every Sunday assisted his disabled mother so lovingly, an active church member who had volunteered for 17 years as the church's treasurer—was in jail, awaiting prosecution.

What was he in trouble for? Stealing money from the church.

Sims told the members about the church's messy accounting, about the threats to turn off the utilities—gas, electricity, water.

Then someone asked, "How much is left?"

Sims cleared his throat, hesitating before the aging congregation. He took in their puzzled, pained looks. He sucked in a deep breath, then delivered the final blow.

"Almost nothing."

Except for $1,800, everything else from the church's bank accounts was gone (Kavanaugh 2002, A1).

When the treasurer of a local church begins the job, it is usually because that person is good with numbers. Maybe he or she knows a thing or two about keeping electronic records. Maybe it's just because this individual is responsible, and the pastor knows that of any position in the church, this one requires someone who is very responsible.

For those who take the job with little previous experience, it isn't long before they begin asking some big questions: "How do we pay the taxes around here?" "What is the process for creating the budget?" "Am I responsible for all of this?"

And for some, like Kent Skidmore, many important questions are never asked. Maybe no one has ever asked questions such as, "Do we need policies about how the money is counted?" and "Is there any special way we need to handle depositing the money?" Thomas Sims can tell you how important those unasked questions are. At the First Presbyterian Church of North Kansas City some people used to count the money alone. Some people took the bank deposits home instead of directly to the bank. And some people are facing over 60 years in prison because the questions never came up until it was too late.

New church treasurers typically approach the job as their service to the church. Thoughts of how to protect themselves and the pastor from the temptation or the appearance of financial misconduct don't always occur until problems arise.

While this kit is useful for the experienced church treasurer who wants a better understanding of the job, it is particularly designed for newer treasurers who have little background in church budgeting or in paying the taxes for a nonprofit organization.

As we interviewed local treasurers for this project, we heard over and over again of the confusing nature of budgeting and reporting, of the tension between pastor and treasurer over items such as ministerial compensation, and what many local congregations do to protect themselves from financial misconduct. But the biggest area of concern to most church treasurers is the issue of paying taxes and reporting to the IRS.

This manual is intended to provide an overview of the job of the

Introduction

local church treasurer and offers tips and suggestions from sources in many denominations. It is also intended to help treasurers know where to go to find answers to their questions. Sometimes this can be as confusing as wrestling the questions themselves. This book is not intended to replace the guidance or policies of your denomination, nor is it intended to give specific legal advice. Treasurers are cautioned that the publisher is not rendering legal, accounting, or other professional services. For answers to specific tax questions, the treasurer should seek the advice of a tax accountant, lawyer, or preparer.

1
RESPONSIBILITIES OF THE CHURCH TREASURER

▶ The church treasurer holds an office of vital importance to the success of the local church ministry. The treasurer represents the church in an official capacity within the church body and outside the church body (e.g., banks, vendors, etc.). In conjunction with the pastor, the treasurer has the critical role of maintaining the business integrity (both in financial and legal matters) of that local body. It is important for the treasurer to stay current on federal, state, and local laws that affect the church with regard to taxes, reporting and filing requirements, and other legal issues.

In most churches in the United States, the church treasurer position is a volunteer, nonpaid staff position. In larger churches, treasurers sometmes receive some compensation. In the largest of churches, the treasurer position is only a position on the church board, with financial duties handled by paid staff such as a church business administrator. A well-informed, conscientious treasurer is often the key for a church desiring to demonstrate accountability and integrity.

The responsibilities of the treasurer should always be in writing, such as in a position description (denominations generally detail church treasurer responsibilities in polity documents). These responsibilities often include the following:

- Serves as financial officer of the congregation ✽
- Is responsible for payment of all bills, invoices, and charges

---

✽With some modification and/or additions, text prefaced by this symbol and parenthetically documented at end is excerpted with permission from the Evangelical Lutheran Church of America, *Resources for Congregational Treasurers and Bookkeepers*, http://www.elca.org/treasurer/congregations/responsibilities.html (accessed April 25, 2008).

- Performs or oversees all of the financial recordkeeping functions
- Prepares the financial reports for the church board and provides appropriate financial information to the church and gift acknowledgments to donors
- Files all of the required federal, state, and local tax forms
- Monitors the cash position of the congregation and invests available funds in accordance with church investment policies
- Is empowered to borrow funds as directed by the church board
- Assists in the preparation of the annual church budget
- Often serves as a member of the church finance committee, if the church has such a committee (Evangelical Lutheran 2007, chapter 1)

SEPARATION OF FINANCIAL RESPONSIBILITIES

The segregation of church financial responsibilities is fundamental to accountability and integrity. While a church treasurer could feel the separation of duties is a negative reflection on the treasurer's trustworthiness, this arrangement is important for the protection of the treasurer and the congregation. The credibility of the church treasurer is vital to the integrity of the church's financial processes. Thus it is critical to protect the treasurer's credibility by establishing appropriate checks and balances.

While church revenue comes in various forms (including rent and fees), offerings are the financial lifeblood of a church. Most offerings received by churches are unrestricted—that is, they may be used to fund any aspect of church ministry. But nearly every church receives some donor-restricted funds, which require special treatment in recording the income and expense.

Why do problems arise in handling church offerings? It is primarily because cash is so easily misappropriated. It is small, lacks owner identification, and has immediate transferability. This is why cash should always be counted and recorded by two people. Sole access to offerings, as will be shown, can create a difficult situation for some people.

Responsibilities of the Church Treasurer

All funds received by a church should be recorded in a way that reflects the nature of the funds, the name of the donor/payer (when available), and the amount donated or paid. Counting forms (similar to the "Offering Counting Form" found on page 127 and the accompanying CD) should be used by tellers to record offering details. The Guidelines for Handling Church Offerings (below) are an excellent basis for developing guidelines specific to the needs of your church.

The following procedures should be conducted *separately* from the treasurer's responsibility:

- Oversight of the counting process
- Oversight of the depositing of all receipts
- Training individuals involved in counting the offering

Offering totals should be reported to the treasurer for recording in the church financial system. Offering details, including any restricted gifts, should be provided either to the treasurer or to another person designated by the church for posting into the donor management system. (If the church does not use an electronic donor management system, a form similar to the "Individual's Contribution Record" found on page 128 and the accompanying CD may be used.)

Guidelines for Handling Church Offerings*

- **Adopt policies to prevent problems.** Written policies are the ounce of prevention that could avoid serious problems at your church. Adopt a series of detailed policies that outline the procedures to be followed from the time the money goes into the offering plate—in worship services, during Sunday School classes, in other services, from the mail, or from delivery to the church—until the money is deposited in the bank.
- **Make accountability and confidentiality dual goals.** Too

---

*This section was reprinted by permission from *The Zondervan Church and Nonprofit Tax & Financial Guide: 2008 Edition* by Dan Busby, CPA (Grand Rapids: Zondervan, 2007), 120-22.

many churches focus so much on confidentiality that accountability takes too low a priority. True, some confidentiality is sacrificed when good accountability exists. But the church that does not balance confidentiality and accountability is treading on dangerous ground.

- **Use confidentiality statements.** Counters should sign a written statement of confidentiality before participating in the counting process. If the commitment of confidentiality is broken, the individual(s) should be removed from the team of counters.

- **Always follow the principle of two.** When a church leaves the offering in control of a single person—even for a short time period—before the count has been recorded or the uncounted offering has been dropped at the bank, it is a blatant invitation for problems. When sole access to the offering is allowed, most people will not take any money. However, for some, the temptation may be too great.

Even when the principle of joint control is carefully followed, collusion between the two people is still possible—leading to a loss of funds. The risk of collusion can be reduced by rotating ushers and offering counters so they don't serve on consecutive weeks. Church treasurers, financial secretaries, and other church-elected individuals should serve for limited terms, such as two or three years. A pastor or the church treasurer should not be involved in the counting process. A husband and wife could serve on the same counting team only if a third party is always present.

Example: The Sunday offerings go from the ushers to the head usher and then to the financial secretary, who takes the money, makes the initial count, records the donations by donor, and then makes the bank deposit. Problem: This violates the principle of having offerings in the control of two individuals until they are counted. The head usher and financial secretary both have the opportunity to remove cash. Or they could be accused of mishandling the funds and have no system of controls to support their innocence.

- **Keep the offering plates in plain view.** When the offering is being received, it is important that each offering plate always be kept in plain view of two ushers. When a solo usher takes an offering plate down a hall, upstairs to the balcony, behind a curtain, or out a door, there is a possibility of losing cash from the plate.
- **Be sure the guidelines cover Sunday School offerings.** Too often churches are very careful with offerings from the worship services but not so careful with offerings received in church school classes. These offerings should be counted in the class and turned over to an usher or counting team comprised of at least two individuals.
- **Encourage the use of offering envelopes.** Members should be encouraged to use offering envelopes. The envelopes provide a basis for recording contributions in the church's donor records.

    Some churches emphasize this concept by providing each individual or church family with a series of prenumbered offering envelopes to be used throughout the calendar year. The numbering system identifies the donor. This can ease the process of posting donations and is an excellent approach.
- **Count the offerings as soon as possible.** A frequent reason given by churches for not counting offerings immediately is that church members don't want to miss the service. This is very understandable. In some churches, the Sunday offerings are counted on Monday. Adequate control over the money is maintained by providing a secure place to store the funds, usually a safe, and carefully limiting access to the storage location.

    However, the greater the length of time between receiving and counting the offering, the greater the potential for the mishandling of funds. When offerings are immediately counted, secure storing of the funds is important but not as critical because an audit trail has been established.

- **Have counters complete offering tally sheets.** Tally sheets should be completed that separately account for loose checks and cash that were placed in offering envelopes. Checks or cash placed in blank, unidentified offering envelopes should be recorded with the loose funds. This separation of money serves as a control amount for the later posting to donor records.

- **Use a secure area for counting.** For the safety of the counting team, confidentiality, and the avoidance of interruptions, provide a secure area in which the offering can be counted. (When offerings are significant, consider providing armed security when offerings are transported to the bank.) The counters should have an adding machine, coin wrappers, offering tally sheets, and other supplies. The adding machine should have a tape (instead of a paperless calculator) so the counting team can run two matching adding machine tapes of the offering.

- **Deposit all offerings intact.** Offerings should always be counted and deposited intact. Depositing intact means not allowing cash in the offering to be used for the payment of church expenses or to be exchanged for other cash or a check.

    If offerings are not deposited intact, an unidentified variance between the count and the deposit could occur. Additionally, if an individual is permitted to cash a check from offering funds, the church may inadvertently provide the person with a cancelled check that could be used in claiming a charitable tax deduction.

- **Verify amounts on offering envelopes with the contents.** As the counting team removes the contents from offering

Responsibilities of the Church Treasurer

envelopes, any amounts written on the envelope by the donors should be compared with the contents. Any variances should be noted on the envelope.

- **Properly identify donor-restricted funds.** All donor restrictions should be carefully preserved during the counting process. These restrictions are usually noted on an offering envelope, but they can take the form of an instruction attached to a check or simply a notation on the check.
- **Use a restrictive endorsement for checks.** During the counting process, it is important to add a restrictive endorsement, with a "For Deposit Only" stamp, to the back of all checks.
- **Place offerings in a secure location when they are stored in the church.** If offerings are stored in the church, even for short periods of time, the use of a secure location is important. A safe implies security, while an unlocked desk drawer connotes lack of security. But defining security is often not that easy.

Again, the principle is that no one person should have access to the funds at any time. This can be accomplished by

- obtaining a safe with two locks
- changing the combination and distributing portions of the new combination to different people or
- placing the safe in a locked room or building and placing the offerings in locked bags before locking them in the safe

Ideally, offerings are counted during or after the service and a deposit is made immediately. Alternately, the cash portion of the offering is recorded and the uncounted offerings are immediately transported to the bank drop box by two people. When these two preferable options are not used, the offerings are generally stored at the church for a period of time on Sunday or perhaps until Monday morning.

This process requires a secure storage location, preferably a safe, and highly structured controls over access to locked bank bags and the safe.

- **Use proper controls when dropping uncounted funds at the bank.** If your church drops uncounted offerings at the bank, several key principles should be followed:
  - The funds should be placed in locked bank bags with careful control of the number of persons who have keys to the bags.
  - Two individuals should transport the funds to the bank.
  - Two people should pick up the funds from the bank on the next business day, count the funds, and make the deposit.
- **Control deposit variances.** Provide written instructions to the bank concerning procedures to be followed if the bank discovers a discrepancy in the deposit. The notification should go to someone other than the individual(s) who participated in preparation of the deposit.
- **Segregate duties when recording individual contributions.** Someone other than a member of the counting team should record individual gifts in donor records. This segregation of duties reduces the possibility of the misappropriation of gifts.

Acknowledging and Reporting Charitable Gifts*

Contributors to your church seeking a federal income tax charitable contribution deduction must produce, if asked, a written receipt from the church if a single contribution's value is $250 or more. Strictly speaking, the burden of compliance with the

---

*This section was reprinted, with minor adaptation, by permission from *The Zondervan Church and Nonprofit Tax & Financial Guide: 2008 Edition* by Dan Busby, CPA (Grand Rapids: Zondervan, 2007), 162-75.

Responsibilities of the Church Treasurer

$250 or more rule falls on the donor. In reality, the burden and administrative costs fall on the church, not the donor.

The IRS can fine a church that deliberately issues a false acknowledgment to a contributor. The fine is up to $1,000 if the donor is an individual and $10,000 if the donor is a corporation.

A donor will not be allowed a charitable deduction for single donations by check or gifts-in-kind of $250 or more unless the donor has an acknowledgment from your church.

If a donor makes multiple contributions of $250 or more to one church, one acknowledgment that reflects the total amount of the donor's contributions to the church for the year is sufficient. In other words, the church can total all of the contributions for a donor and only show the total amount on the receipt.

If a donor contributes cash, the donor must have an acknowledgment to qualify for a charitable deduction—this is true for all cash gifts without regard to whether they are single gifts of $250 or more.

- **Information to be included in the receipt.** The following information must be included in the gift receipt:
    - the donor's name
    - if cash, the amount of cash contributed
    - if property, a description, but not the value (if the gift is an auto, boat, or airplane, the church must generally provide Form 1098-C to the donor), of the property
    - a statement explaining whether the church provided any goods or services to the donor in exchange for the contribution
    - if goods or services were provided to the donor, a description and good-faith estimate of their value and a statement that the donor's charitable deduction is limited to the amount of the payment in excess of the value of the goods and services provided, and if services were provided consisting solely of intangible religious benefits, a statement to that effect

- the date the donation was made and
- the date the receipt was issued

- **When receipts should be issued.** Donors must obtain their receipts no later than the due date, plus any extension, of their income tax returns or the date the return is filed, whichever date is earlier. If a donor receives the receipt after this date, the gift does not qualify for a contribution deduction even on an amended return.

  If your church is issuing receipts on an annual basis, you should try to get them to your donors by at least January 31 each year and earlier in January if possible. This will assist your donors in gathering the necessary data for tax return preparation.

  Form 1098-C must be provided within 30 days after the date that [a donated] vehicle is sold or within 30 days of the donation date if the church keeps the property.

- **Frequency of issuing receipts.** The receipts or acknowledgments can be issued gift-by-gift, monthly, quarterly, annually, or any other frequency. For ease of administration and clear communication with donors, many churches provide a receipt for all gifts, whether more or less than $250.

- **Form of receipts.** Except for Form 1098-C, used for gifts of autos, boats, or airplanes, no specific design of the receipt is required. The IRS has not issued any sample receipts to follow.

  The receipt can be a letter, a postcard, or a computer-generated form. It does not have to include the donor's social security number or other taxpayer identification number. A receipt can also be provided electronically, such as via an e-mail addressed to the donor.

- **Separate gifts of less than $250.** If a donor makes separate gifts by check during a calendar year of less than $250, there is no receipting requirement since each gift is a separate contribution. The donor's cancelled check will provide sufficient substantiation. However, most churches receipt all gifts with no distinction between the gifts under or over $250.

- **Donations payable to another charity.** A church member may place a check in the offering plate of $250 or more payable to a mission organization designed for the support of a particular missionary serving with the mission. In this instance, no receipting is required by your church. Since the check was payable to the mission agency, that entity will need to issue the acknowledgment to entitle the donor to claim the gift as a charitable contribution.
- **Donor's out-of-pocket expenses.** You may have volunteers who incur out-of-pocket expenses on behalf of your church. Substantiation from your church is required if a volunteer claims a deduction for unreimbursed expenses of $250 or more. However, the IRS acknowledges that the church may be unaware of the details of the expenses or the dates on which they were incurred. Therefore, the church must substantiate only the types of services performed by the volunteer that relate to out-of-pocket expenses.
- **Individuals.** Gifts made to poor or needy individuals ordinarily do not qualify as charitable contributions. Gifts made personally to employees of a church are not charitable contributions.
- **Foreign organizations.** Earmarked gifts are not limited to gifts earmarked for individuals; a gift may be earmarked for an organization. It may be inappropriate to accept gifts restricted for a foreign charity even if the charitable purposes of the foreign charity are consistent with the purposes of the church.

    Example 1: An individual offers to make a $5,000 donation to your church restricted for the Sri Lanka Relief Outreach for its relief and development purposes, a foreign charity. While the church provides funding for various foreign missionary endeavors, it has no connection with the Sri Lanka Relief Outreach and has no practical way to provide due diligence in relation to a gift to this entity. Based on these facts, the gift has the characteristics of an earmarked gift. The funds should generally not be accepted by the church.

Example 2: Same fact pattern as in Example 1, except the church regularly sponsors short-term mission trips to Sri Lanka and provides funds to the Sri Lanka Relief Outreach, based on the due diligence performed by the church's staff and volunteers on mission trips with respect to this particular foreign entity. Based on these facts, the church is generally in a sound position to make a gift of $5,000 to the Sri Lanka-based charity as requested by the donor, avoiding the characteristics of earmarking.

Since gifts by U.S. taxpayers to a foreign charity do not produce a charitable deduction, donors may earmark a gift for a foreign charity to try to convince a church to pass it through to the entity. When a church is empowered in such a way that it is no more than an agent of or trustee for a particular foreign organization, has purposes so narrow that its funds can go only to a particular foreign organization, or solicits funds on behalf of a particular foreign organization, the deductibility of gifts may be questioned by the IRS.

- **Contingencies.** If a contribution will not be effective until the occurrence of a certain event, an income tax charitable deduction generally is not allowable until the occurrence of the event.

    Example: A donor makes a gift to a church to fund a new education program that the church does not presently offer and is not contemplating. The donation would not be deductible until the church agrees to the conditions of the gift.

Most gifts do not require any reporting by the church to the IRS. In addition to gifts of autos, boats, and airplanes, certain gifts

Responsibilities of the Church Treasurer

require IRS reporting, or execution of a form that the donor files with the IRS:

- **Gifts of property in excess of $5,000.** Substantiation requirements apply to contributions of property (other than money and publicly traded securities) if the total claimed or reported value of the property is more than $5,000. For these gifts, the donor must obtain a qualified appraisal and attach an appraisal summary to the return on which the deduction is claimed. There is an exception for nonpublicly traded stock. If the claimed value of the stock does not exceed $10,000 but is greater than $5,000, the donor does not have to obtain an appraisal by a qualified appraiser.

  The appraisal summary must be on Form 8283, signed and dated by the church and the appraiser, and attached to the donor's return on which a deduction is claimed. The signature by the church does not represent concurrence in the appraised value of the contributed property.

  If Form 8283 is required, it is the donor's responsibility to file it. The church is under no responsibility to see that donors file this form or that it is properly completed. However, advising donors of their obligations and providing them with the form can produce donor goodwill.

- **Gifts of property in excess of $500.** Gifts of property valued at $500 or more require the completion of certain information on page 1 of Form 8283. For gifts between $500 and $5,000 in value, there is no requirement of an appraisal or signature of the church.

- **Charity reporting for contributed property.** If property received as a charitable contribution requiring an appraisal summary on Form 8283 is sold, exchanged, or otherwise disposed of by the church within three years after the date of its contribution, the church must file Form 8282 with the IRS within 125 days of the disposition.

  This form provides detailed information on the gift and

the disposal of the property. A copy of this information return must be provided to the donor and retained by the church.

A church that receives a charitable contribution valued at more than $5,000 from a corporation generally does not have to complete Form 8283.

A letter or other written communication from a church acknowledging receipt of the property and showing the name of the donor, the date and location of the contribution, and a detailed description of the property is an acceptable contribution receipt for a gift of property.

There is no requirement to include the value of contributed property on the receipt. A tension often surrounds a significant gift of property because the donor may request the church to include an excessively high value on the charitable receipt. It is wise for the church to remain impartial in the matter and simply acknowledge the property by description and condition while excluding a dollar amount.

> *Example:* A church receives a gift of real estate. The receipt should include the legal description of the real property and a description of the improvements with no indication of the dollar value.

- **Acknowledging and reporting gifts of autos, boats, and airplanes.** Churches are required to provide contemporaneous written acknowledgment containing specific information to donors of autos, boats, and airplanes. Taxpayers are required to include a copy of the written acknowledgments with their tax returns in order to receive a deduction. The church is also required to provide the information contained in the acknowledgment to the IRS. The information included in such acknowledgments as well as the meaning of "contemporaneous" depends on what the church does with the donated vehicle.

    Vehicle sold before use or improvement. If the donat-

Responsibilities of the Church Treasurer

ed auto, boat, or airplane is sold before significant intervening use or material improvement of the auto, boat, or airplane by the organization, the gross proceeds received by the church from the sale of the vehicle will be included on the written acknowledgment. Therefore, for donated property sold before use or improvement, the deductible amount is the gross proceeds received from the sale.

For property sold before use or improvement, a written acknowledgment is considered contemporaneous if the church provides it within 30 days of the sale of the vehicle. The written acknowledgment provided by the church should include the following information:

- the name and taxpayer identification number of the donor
- the vehicle, boat, or airplane identification number or similar number
- certification that the property was sold in an arm's-length transaction between unrelated parties
- the gross proceeds from the sale and
- a statement that the deductible amount may not exceed the amount of the gross proceeds

If a church furnishes a false or fraudulent acknowledgment or fails to furnish an acknowledgment in accordance with the time and content requirements, the church will be subject to a penalty equal to the greater of

- the product of the highest rate of tax and the sales price stated on the acknowledgment or
- the gross proceeds from the sale of the property

Vehicle not sold before use or improvement. Churches may plan to significantly use or materially improve a donated auto, boat, or airplane before or instead of selling the property. In such circumstances, the church would not include a dollar amount in the written acknowledgment. Instead, the written acknowledgment (written within 30 days

of the contribution of the vehicle to be considered contemporaneous) should include the following information (Form 1098-C may be used as the acknowledgment):
- the name and taxpayer identification number of the donor
- the vehicle, boat, or airplane identification number or similar number
- certification of the intended use or material improvement of the property and the intended duration of such use and
- certification that the property will not be transferred in exchange for money, other property, or services before completion of such use or improvement

The deductible amount for contributed autos, boats, or airplanes that will be used or improved by the church is the fair market value of the property, as determined by the donor, taking into consideration accessories, mileage, and other indicators of the property's general condition.

For donated autos, boats, or airplanes that a church will use or improve, if a donee organization furnishes a false or fraudulent acknowledgment or fails to furnish an acknowledgment in accordance with the time and content requirements, the church will be subject to a penalty equal to the greater of
- the product of the highest rate of tax and the claimed value of the property or
- $5,000

In certain instances, an auto, boat, or airplane may be sold at a price significantly below fair market value (or gratuitously transferred) to needy individuals in direct furtherance of the church's charitable purpose (although it is difficult to imagine how a boat or an airplane would meet this definition).

For property that meets this definition, the gift acknowledgment also must contain a certification that the church will sell the property to a needy individual at a price significantly below fair market value (or, if applicable, that the church gratuitously will transfer the property to a needy individual) and that the sale or transfer will be in the direct furtherance of the church's charitable purpose of relieving the poor and distressed or the underprivileged who are in need of a means of transportation.

Example: On March 1, 2008, a donor contributes a qualified vehicle to a church. The church's charitable purposes include helping needy individuals who are unemployed develop new job skills, finding job placements for these individuals, and providing transportation for these individuals who need a means of transportation to jobs in areas not served by public transportation. The church determines that, in direct furtherance of its charitable purpose, the church will sell the qualified vehicle at a price significantly below fair market value to a trainee who needs a means of transportation to a new workplace. On or before March 31, 2008, the church provides Form 1098-C to the donor containing the donor's name and taxpayer identification number, the vehicle identification number, a statement that the date of the contribution was March 1, 2008, a certification that the church will sell the qualified vehicle to a needy individual at a price significantly below fair market value, and a certification that the sale is in direct furtherance of the church's charitable purpose.

Generally, no deduction is allowed unless donors receive Form 1098-C within 30 days after the date that the vehicle is sold or within 30 days of the donation date if the church keeps the car. If the vehicle is sold, donors must be informed of the gross selling price.

If the church keeps the car, the private-party sale price

must be used by donors to figure the charitable tax deduction for donations, not the higher dealer retail price.

(See "Sample Charitable Gift Receipt" No. 1 and "Sample Letter to Noncash Donors" in Appendix 2 and on the accompanying CD.)

Quid Pro Quo Disclosure Requirements*

When a donor receives goods or services of value approximate to the amount transferred, there is no gift. This is because the person received a quid pro quo in exchange for the transfer, and thus, there is no gift at all. If the payment to a church exceeds the approximate amount of goods or services provided to the payor, the difference qualifies as a charitable gift.

The church is required to provide a receipt for all transactions where the donor makes a payment of more than $75 to the church and receives goods or services (other than intangible religious benefits or items of token value).

Form of the Receipt

The receipt must
- inform the donor that the amount of the contribution that is deductible for federal income tax purposes is limited to the difference in the amount of money and the value of any property contributed by the donor over the value of the goods or services provided by the church and
- provide the donor with a good-faith estimate of the value of goods or services that the church is providing in exchange for the contribution

Only single payments of more than $75 are subject to the rules. Payments are not cumulative. It is not a difference of $75 between the amount given by the donor and the value of the ob-

---

*This section was reprinted, with minor adaptation, by permission from *The Zondervan Church and Nonprofit Tax & Financial Guide: 2008 Edition* by Dan Busby, CPA (Grand Rapids: Zondervan, 2007), 175–80.

ject received by the donor that triggers the disclosure requirements, but the amount actually paid by the donor.

Calculating the Gift Portion

It is not a requirement for the church to actually complete the subtraction of the benefit from a cash payment, showing the net charitable deduction. However, providing the net amount available for a charitable deduction is a good approach for clear communication with your donors.

When to Make the Required Disclosures

The disclosure of the value of goods or services provided to a donor may be made in the donor solicitation as well as in the subsequent receipt. However, sufficient information will generally not be available to make proper disclosure upon solicitation. For example, the value of a dinner may not be known at the time the solicitation is made.

Goods Provided to Donors

To determine the net charitable contribution, a gift must generally be reduced by the fair market value of any premium, incentive, or other benefit received by the donor in exchange for the gift. Common examples of premiums are books, tapes, and Bibles.

For gifts of over $75, organizations must advise the donor of the fair market value of the premium or incentive and explain that the value is not deductible for tax purposes.

Donors must reduce their charitable deduction by the fair market value of goods or services they receive even when the goods or services were donated to the church for use as premiums or gifts or when they were bought wholesale by the church. Therefore, churches cannot pass along to donors the savings realized by receiving products at no cost or buying products at a discount.

If donors receive benefits of insubstantial value, they are allowed a full tax deduction for the donation:

- **Low-cost items.** If an item that has a cost (not retail value) of

less than $9.10 and bears the name or logo of your church is given in return for a donation of more than $45.50 (2008 inflation-adjusted amount), the donor may claim a charitable deduction for the full amount of the donation. Examples of items that often qualify as tokens are coffee mugs, key chains, bookmarks, and calendars.
- **De minimis benefits.** A donor can take a full deduction if the fair market value of the benefits received in connection with a gift does not exceed 2 percent of the donation or $91 (2008 inflation-adjusted amount), whichever is less.

Examples of the Quid Pro Quo Rules

Here are various examples of how the quid pro quo rules apply:

- **Admission to events.** Many churches sponsor banquets, concerts, or other events to which donors and prospective donors are invited in exchange for a contribution or other payment. Often, the donor receives a benefit equivalent to the payment and no charitable deduction is available.

  But if the amount paid is more than the value received, the amount in excess of the fair market value is deductible if the donor intended to make a contribution.

- **Auctions.** The IRS generally takes the position that the fair market value of an item purchased at a church auction is set by the bidders. The winning bidder, therefore, cannot pay more than the item is worth. That means there is no charitable contribution in the IRS's eyes, no deduction, and no need for the church to provide any charitable gift substantiation document to the bidder.

  However, many tax professionals take the position that when the payment (the purchase price) exceeds the fair market value of the items, the amount that exceeds the fair market value is deductible as a charitable contribution. This position also creates a reporting requirement under the quid

Responsibilities of the Church Treasurer

pro quo rules. Most churches set the value of every object sold and provide receipts to buyers.

Example: Your church youth group auctions goods to raise funds for a missions trip. An individual bought a quilt for $200. The church takes the position that the quilt had a fair market value of $50 even though the bidder paid $200. Since the payment of $200 exceeded the $75 limit, the church is required to provide a written statement indicating that only $150 of the $200 payment is eligible for a charitable contribution.

- **Bazaars.** Payments for items sold at bazaars and bake sales are not tax deductible to donors since the purchase price generally equals the fair market value of the item.
- **Banquets.** Whether your church incurs reporting requirements in connection with banquets where funds are raised depends on the specifics of each event.

    Example 1: Your church sponsors a banquet for missions charging $50 per person. The meal costs the church $15 per person. There is no disclosure requirement since the amount charged was less than $75. However, the amount deductible by each donor is only $35.

    Example 2: Your church invites individuals to attend a missions banquet without charge. Attendees are invited to make contributions or pledges at the end of the banquet. These payments probably do not require disclosure even if the amount given is $75 or more because there is only an indirect relationship between the meal and the gift.

- **Deduction timing.** Goods or services received in consideration for a donor's payment include goods and services received in a different year. Thus, a donor's deduction for the year of the payment is limited to the amount, if any, by which

the payment exceeds the value of the goods and services.
- **Good-faith estimates.** A donor is not required to use the estimate provided by a church in calculating the deductible amount. When a taxpayer knows or has reason to know that an estimate is inaccurate, the taxpayer may ignore the church's estimate.
- **Rights of refusal.** A donor can claim a full deduction if he or she refuses a benefit from the church. However, this must be done affirmatively. Simply not taking advantage of a benefit is not enough. For example, a donor who chooses not to make use of tickets made available by your church must deduct the value of the tickets from his or her contribution before claiming a deduction. However, a donor who rejects the right to a benefit at the time the contribution is made (e.g., by checking off a refusal box on a form supplied by your charity) can take a full deduction.
- **Sale of products or a service at fair market value.** When an individual purchases products or receives services approximate to the amount paid, no part of the payment is a gift.

    Example 1: An individual purchases tapes of a series of Sunday morning worship services for $80. The sales price represents fair market value. Even though the amount paid exceeds the $75 threshold, the church is not required to provide a disclosure statement to the purchaser because the value of the products is approximate to the amount paid to the church.

    Example 2: The Brown family uses the fellowship hall of the church for a family reunion. The normal rental fee is $300. The Browns give a check to the church for $300 marked "Contribution." No receipt should be given because no charitable contribution was made. The Browns received a benefit approximate to the amount of their payment.

Example 3: The Brown family uses the church sanctuary and fellowship hall for a wedding and the reception. The church does not have a stated use fee but asks for a donation from those who use the facility. The comparable fee to rent similar facilities is $250. The Browns give a check to the church for $250 marked "Contribution." No receipt should be given because no charitable contribution was made. The Browns received a benefit approximate to the amount of their payment. Note: It is inappropriate for the church to try to mask a fee by calling it a donation.

Example 4: Your church operates a Christian school. The parent of a student at the school writes a check payable to the church for his child's tuition. No receipt should be given because a payment of tuition does not qualify as a charitable contribution.

(For examples of these types of contribution receipts, see "Sample Charitable Gift Receipt" No. 2 in Appendix 2 and on the accompanying CD.)

Suggested Steps in Handling Expenditures

1. Bills and obligations should be approved for payment based on a Travel and Other Expense Reimbursement Policy (see Appendix 2 and accompanying CD). This approval should be indicated in writing by the person responsible. In larger congregations, a purchase approval form may be used to approve a payment and identify the account to be charged. In all cases, expenditures should be supported by original invoices and/or receipts, not photocopies.
2. Check is prepared.
3. Check is signed by person(s) authorized under the bank account agreement. The pastor should not be an authorized signer. In order to prevent delays in payment when the treasurer is not available, churches should have multiple

people authorized for the signing of checks under the bank agreement.
4. Blank checks should never be signed in advance, under any circumstance.
5. The check number is written on the invoice or support document to prevent duplicate payments, and the check is mailed.
6. If the financial secretary and/or treasurer is authorized to initiate fund transfers to or from savings and/or investment accounts via telephone, it is suggested that a verification notice (written form) be developed indicating that on a specific date such a transfer took place, including the purpose, and signed by the chair of the church's governing board. This form should be retained in the files of these accounts (Evangelical Lutheran 2007, chapter 3).

Other Forms of Payment

If your church adopts the policy that all payments, other than minor payments through a properly established petty cash fund, be paid by check, the treasurer's job of recording all expenses is much easier and you will avoid many of the pitfalls associated with alternative means of purchasing, such as credit cards.

Credit Cards

When a church uses the credit card method of payment, those with the main purchasing responsibilities in the various departments may request the privilege of using the church's card for approved expenses. While this system simplifies the jobs of these persons in that they do not have to submit their purchase needs in advance, it can easily get out of hand. For example, some people in the local church do not always share the treasurer's level of commitment to saving proper documentation of ministry expenses that is necessary for tax deductions. It is not uncommon for the treasurers who work in churches that use credit cards to be completely uninformed of some expenses until the credit card bill

Responsibilities of the Church Treasurer

arrives. Upon receiving the bill, the treasurer must track down all expenses shown on the credit card statement and collect the documentation after the fact. This same problem often occurs in churches where each department has its own checkbook, with the treasurer knowing nothing of the expenses until the bank statement arrives.

Another significant challenge for churches that use credit cards involves the short turnaround time credit card companies give for submitting payment on a bill. The time for the treasurer to track down, document, and get proper authorization signatures does not always allow time for the credit card bills to be paid by the due date. Credit card companies generally charge fees for late payments. These fees can add up quickly.

The simplest answer to this challenge is to have only *approved* individuals purchase what they need and submit their receipts for reimbursement. "Approved" is emphasized because it is important to keep potential expenses within reason. One approach is to have only one person in each department authorized to approve expenses. This plan eliminates numerous individuals approaching the treasurer seeking reimbursement for dubious expenses from which the church may not benefit.

Using credit cards comes not without challenges. To successfully meet these challenges churches should adopt credit card policies and procedures and have each cardholder sign an agreement to abide by them. Churches can then benefit from the conveniences that credit cards bring while establishing proper safeguards for their use.

(See the "Sample Credit Card Policies and Procedures" and "Church Cardholder Agreement" in Appendix 2 and on the accompanying CD.)

SHOULD YOU COMPUTERIZE YOUR ✱ CHURCH'S FINANCIAL RECORDS?

The availability of the computer provides the means to establish an accounting system that offers everything a congregation may require for the recording and processing of its financial information.

The software program for this accounting process should be a double-entry system. Many small churches use entry-level software, such as QuickBooks. As a church grows, it should consider purchasing a higher level software to more adequately handle budgeting, reporting, payroll, and more.

It should provide for check writing and a monthly reconciliation of deposits and withdrawals (canceled checks). Since this type of accounting software automatically records deposits and disbursements as posted to the congregation's chart of accounts, the ability to create reports of financial activity is relatively easy and can provide informative details of the congregation's financial status as related to its annual budget program. (Evangelical Lutheran 2007, chapter 5).

2

PAYROLL, EMPLOYEES, AND MINISTERIAL COMPENSATION*

Dear Sirs:
The only employee we have besides our pastor is a part-time custodian [or secretary]. Do you know of any way we could pay our part-time employee by contract and save the trouble of withholding income taxes and social security/Medicare (FICA) taxes?

In one form or another this question has been asked literally hundreds of times in financial seminars, correspondence, and telephone conversations. The question comes as a response to the increasing responsibilities of churches and other employers for reporting employee compensation information to the IRS. Fortunately, the answer is fairly straightforward. However, it is frequently not the answer desired by the questioner (Pensions n.d., Memo 2).

WHO IS AN EMPLOYEE, AND WHO IS A CONTRACTOR?

A congregation typically has a number of individuals it pays for services. The most important consideration is to determine whether the individual is an employee or is self-employed (a contractor).

---

*Special thanks to Pensions and Benefits USA for their excellent work that comprises a great deal of this chapter. Due to the continual changes that occur in the United States tax code, part of Pensions' ministry is to keep church treasurers apprised of the most recent changes that affect churches. For updates to the material presented in this chapter, visit the Pensions and Benefits Web site at pensions.nazarene.org.

Employees

There are basically two types of employees defined by the tax code: statutory employees and common-law employees. Statutory employees have specifically defined jobs that on the surface might appear to be self-employed positions were it not for the statutes that define the work as that of an employee. The common-law employee is the category that affects local churches most often.

A common-law employee is generally anyone who performs services that can be controlled by the employer. That is, the employer has the legal right to control (even if it's not enforced) the means, methods, and results of the services provided. If the employer-employee relationship is deemed to exist based on the facts in each case, it does not matter what it is called, how the payments are measured or paid, nor if the services are performed full-time or part-time. The employer must determine any taxable amounts paid, withhold appropriate taxes for lay employees, make appropriate tax payments, and report those taxes to the IRS. Virtually all pastors, associate ministers, church custodians, church secretaries, paid choir directors, paid nursery workers, and so on, are viewed by the IRS as common-law employees. Their compensation is reported on Form W-2 (Pensions n.d., Memo 2).

> **There are basically two types of employees defined by the tax code: statutory employees and common-law employees.**

As an aid to determine whether an individual is an employee under the common-law rules, 20 factors or elements have been identified as indicating whether sufficient control is present to establish an employer-employee relationship. The 20 factors have been developed based on an examination of cases and rulings considering whether an individual is an employee. The IRS also categorized these factors into three general principles of how an organization may have control over a worker. They are behavioral control, financial control, and the relationship between the organization and the individual.

The importance of each factor varies depending on the occupation and the factual context in which the services are performed. The 20 factors are designed only as guides for determining whether an individual is an employee; special scrutiny is required in applying the 20 factors to assure that the form of an arrangement designed to achieve a particular status does not obscure the substance of the arrangement (i.e., whether the person or persons for whom the services are performed exercise sufficient control over the individual for the individual to be classified as an employee).

The factors[1] are described below and broken down into their respective categories.[2] However, care should also be taken to conform to the emerging seven-part test following these factors.

Behavioral Control

1. **Instructions.** A worker who is required to comply with other persons' instructions about when, where, and how he or she is to work is ordinarily an employee. This control factor is present if the person or persons for whom the services are performed have the *right* to require compliance with instructions. See, for example, *Rev. Rul. 68-598, 1968-2 C.B. 464,* and *Rev. Rul. 66-381, 1966-2 C.B. 449.*

2. **Training.** Training a worker by requiring an experienced employee to work with the worker, by corresponding with the worker, by requiring the worker to attend meetings, or by using other methods, indicates that the person or persons for whom the services are performed want the

---

1. Excerpted from *Revenue Ruling 87-41, 1987-1 C.B. 296.*
2. Note: the factors are rearranged in order to group the factors into their respective categories in order to be applied more easily. David B. Bailey, 16 *Taxation of Exempts* 150 (Jan./Feb. 2005).

services performed in a particular method or manner. See *Rev. Rul. 70-630, 1970-2 C.B. 229.*

3. **Integration.** Integration of the worker's services into the business operations generally shows that the worker is subject to direction and control. When the success or continuation of a business depends to an appreciable degree upon the performance of certain services, the workers who perform those services must necessarily be subject to a certain amount of control by the owner of the business. See *United States v. Silk,* 331 U.S. 704 (1947), *1947-2 C.B. 167, Weber v. Commissioner,* 103 TC 378 (1994).

4. **Order or sequence set.** If a worker must perform services in the order or sequence set by the person or persons for whom the services are performed, that factor shows that the worker is not free to follow the worker's own pattern of work but must follow the established routines and schedules of the person or persons for whom the services are performed. Often, because of the nature of an occupation, the person or persons for whom the services are performed do not set the order of the services or set the order infrequently. It is sufficient to show control, however, if such person or persons retain the right to do so. See *Rev. Rul. 56-69.*

5. **Hiring, supervising, and paying assistants.** If the person or persons for whom the services are performed hire, supervise, and pay assistants, that factor generally shows control over the workers on the job. However, if one worker hires, supervises, and pays the other assistants pursuant to a contract under which the worker agrees to provide materials and labor and under which the worker is responsible only for the attainment of a result, this factor indicates an independent contractor status. Compare *Rev. Rul. 63-115, 1963-1 C.B. 178* with *Rev. Rul. 55-593, 1955-2 C.B. 610.*

Payroll, Employees, and Ministerial Compensation

6. **Furnishing of tools and materials.** The fact that the person or persons for whom the services are performed furnish significant tools, materials, and other equipment tends to show the existence of an employer-employee relationship. See *Rev. Rul. 71-524, 1971-2 C.B. 346.*
7. **Set hours of work.** The establishment of set hours of work by the person or persons for whom the services are performed is a factor indicating control. See *Rev. Rul. 73-591, 1973-2 C.B. 337.*
8. **Full time required.** If the worker must devote substantially full time to the business of the person or persons for whom the services are performed, such person or persons have control over the amount of time the worker spends working and implicitly restrict the worker from doing other gainful work. An independent contractor, on the other hand, is free to work when and for whom he or she chooses. See *Rev. Rul. 56-694, 1956-2 C.B. 694.*
9. **Oral or written reports.** A requirement that the worker submit regular or written reports to the person or persons for whom the services are performed indicates a degree of control. See *Rev. Rul. 70-309, 1970-1 C.B. 199*, and *Rev. Rul. 68-248, 1968-1 C.B. 431*.

Financial Control

10. **Payment by hour, week, or month.** Payment by the hour, week, or month generally points to an employer-employee relationship, provided that this method of payment is not just a convenient way of paying a lump sum agreed upon as the cost of a job. Payment made by the job or on a straight commission generally indicates that the worker is an independent contractor. See *Rev. Rul. 74-389, 1974-2 C.B. 330*.
11. **Significant investment.** If the worker invests in facilities that are used by the worker in performing services and

are not typically maintained by employees (such as the maintenance of an office rented at fair value from an unrelated party), that factor tends to indicate that the worker is an independent contractor. On the other hand, lack of investment in facilities indicates dependence on the person or persons for whom the services are performed for such facilities and, accordingly, the existence of an employer-employee relationship. See *Rev. Rul. 71-524*. Special scrutiny is required with respect to certain types of facilities, such as home offices.

12. **Realization of profit or loss.** A worker who can realize a profit or suffer a loss as a result of the worker's services (in addition to the profit or loss ordinarily realized by employees) is generally an independent contractor, but the worker who cannot is an employee. See *Rev. Rul. 70-309*. For example, if the worker is subject to a real risk of economic loss due to significant investments or a bona fide liability for expenses, such as salary payments to unrelated employees, that factor indicates that the worker is an independent contractor. The risk that a worker will not receive payment for his or her services, however, is common to both independent contractors and employees and thus does not constitute a sufficient economic risk to support treatment as an independent contractor.

13. **Payment of business and/or travel expenses.** If the person or persons for whom the services are performed ordinarily pay the worker's business and/or traveling expenses, the worker is ordinarily an employee. An employer, to be able to control expenses, generally retains the right to regulate and direct the worker's business activities. See *Rev. Rul. 55-144, 1955-1 C.B. 483*.

14. **Making service available to the general public.** The fact that a worker makes his or her services available to the general public on a regular and consistent basis indi-

Payroll, Employees, and Ministerial Compensation

cates an independent contractor relationship. See *Rev. Rul. 56-660.*

15. **Working for more than one firm at a time.** If a worker performs more than de minimis services for a multiple of unrelated persons or firms at the same time, that factor generally indicates that the worker is an independent contractor. See *Rev. Rul. 70-572, 1970-2 C.B. 221.* However, a worker who performs services for more than one person may be an employee of each of the persons, especially where such persons are part of the same service arrangement.

Relationship of the Parties

16. **Right to discharge.** The right to discharge a worker is a factor indicating that the worker is an employee and the person possessing the right is an employer. An employer exercises control through the threat of dismissal, which causes the worker to obey the employer's instructions. An independent contractor, on the other hand, cannot be fired so long as the independent contractor produces a result that meets the contract specifications. See *Rev. Rul. 75-41, 1975-1 C.B. 323.*

17. **Right to terminate.** If the worker has the right to end his or her relationship with the person for whom the services are performed at any time he or she wishes without incurring liability, that factor indicates an employer-employee relationship. See *Rev. Rul. 70-309.*

18. **Continuing relationship.** A continuing relationship between the worker and the person or persons for whom the services are performed indicates that an employer-employee relationship exists. A continuing relationship may exist where work is performed at frequently recurring although irregular intervals. See *United States v. Silk.*

19. **Services rendered personally.** If the services must be rendered personally, presumably the person or persons

for whom the services are performed are interested in the methods used to accomplish the work as well as in the results. See *Rev. Rul. 55-695, 1955-2 C.B. 410.*

20. **Doing work on employer's premises.** If the work is performed on the premises of the person or persons for whom the services are performed, that factor suggests control over the worker, especially if the work could be done elsewhere. See *Rev. Rul. 56-660, 1956-2 C.B. 693.* Work done off the premises of the person or persons receiving the services, such as at the office of the worker, indicates some freedom from control. However, this fact by itself does not mean that the worker is not an employee. The importance of this factor depends on the nature of the service involved and the extent to which an employer generally would require that employees perform such services on the employer's premises. Control over the place of work is indicated when the person or persons for whom the services are performed have the right to compel the worker to travel a designated route, to canvass a territory within a certain time, or to work at specific places as required. See *Rev. Rul. 56-694.*

The IRS published another perspective on the independent contractor versus employee issue in its *Employment Tax Update—Review of Current Litigation,* a part of the Exempt Organizations—Technical Instruction Program for FY 2003. In the document, the IRS differentiated between control and independence by examining behavioral control factors and financial control factors. This is the source of the three categories of factors. The document also provides an update of case law and law review articles over the preceding five years. Some of the cases covered in the publication are listed at the end of this document.

Emerging Test Applied by the Tax Court

The United States Tax Court has applied a modified standard

in determining whether a relationship is that of employee or an independent contractor. This is a 7-factor test that has some overlap with the 20 factors above. As mentioned before, whether an employer-employee relationship exists in a particular situation is a factual question[3] and accordingly must be carefully analyzed on a case-by-case basis. In ambiguous situations there is a presumption of an employer-employee relationship.[4]

1. **Degree of control.** This is considered the "crucial test."[5] The degree of control necessary to find employee status varies with the nature of the services provided by the worker. The emphasis in this test is not on whether there is actual control over how work is accomplished, but rather if there is a right to exert such control. The distinction here is whether the employer has more than a right to dictate the result to be accomplished, such as the means and methods to be used in accomplishing the work. If a relationship would extend beyond this result, then it would be indicative of an employer-employee relationship. Additionally, the fact a worker is able to set his or her own hours is not necessarily indicative that it is an independent contractor relationship, but rather it must be considered in the broader context of the situation.

2. **Investment in facilities.** The emphasis in this factor is examining who is making the investment in plant, property, or equipment in order to accomplish the work. If the worker is not required to make any investment in order to complete the work, then this would be indicative that there is an employer-employee relationship. Additionally, it should be noted that occasionally working from home and using a personal computer to complete the work may not necessarily be sufficient to be considered an independent contractor.

---

3. *Weber v. Commissioner,* 103 T.C. 378, 386 (1994).
4. *Ewens & Miller, Inc. v. Commissioner,* 117 T.C. 263, 269 (2001).
5. *Weber v. Commissioner,* 117 T.C. 378, 387 (1994).

The Tax Court ruled and affirmed this stance especially in cases where this was de minimis and voluntary.

3. **Opportunity for profit or loss.** This factor examines whether the worker has an opportunity to profit or loss beyond hourly wages. If there is no such exposure to risk or loss, then this would be indicative of an employer-employee relationship.
4. **Right to discharge.** This factor examines whether the employer has the right to discharge the employee at any time. If this right exists, this would be consistent with an employer-employee relationship.
5. **Integral part of business.** This factor examines whether the performed work is part of the regular business of the organization. Examples of integral parts of business indicating employee status include filing, photocopying, running errands, and sending mail.
6. **Permanency of the relationship.** This factor examines whether there is a sufficient time in which to create some permanence of the relationship, thus indicating employee status. A transitory work relationship may point toward independent contractor status.[6] However, the mere fact that a worker could leave at any time for a better position is not sufficient to establish an independent contractor relationship.[7]
7. **Relationship the parties thought they created.** This factor looks to the intent of the parties as to what type of relationship was to be created as well as to what formalities were followed in respect to the relationship. These formalities include specifically what tax forms are filed. If an independent contractor relationship is to be formed, then it is important to file Form 1099-MISC for the nonemployee compensation paid to the worker.

---

6. *Ewens & Miller, Inc. v. Commissioner,* 117 T.C. 263, 273 (2001).
7. *Kumpel v. Commissioner,* T.C. Memo 2003-265.

Payroll, Employees, and Ministerial Compensation

Contractors, Employees, and Ministers

Some local churches do hire independent contractors who offer specific services to the general public. Generally, in a year's time an independent contractor will have more than one organization to which he or she offers services. Examples would be services provided by a janitorial service, snow removal service, roofing contractor, and so on, that are advertised citywide.

> What is a general contractor? A general contractor usually has more than one organization to which he or she offers services. See IRS's 20 factors for more help.

No employer-employee relationship exists between the church and a person performing such a service as an independent contractor. There is, however, one important year-end filing requirement. The IRS requires that Form 1099-MISC be prepared and given to the worker in the event that the individual received more than $600 during the course of the year. The church treasurer should also prepare form 1096 and submit it as the cover form for the Form 1099s.

Before any payment is made to an independent contractor, the church should request that the contractor file form W-9 with the church so it can secure the social security number of this individual.

💡 **If the independent contractor is in the business of supplying its services to the general public and advertises such services, it would be appropriate for the church to request a "certificate of insurance" from the contractor naming the church as "additional insured" on the contractor's insurance policy. This would indicate to the church that for this particular project the contractor has liability and workers' compensation insurance in place (Evangelical Lutheran 2007, chapter 9).**

Note: An unincorporated evangelist qualifies as an independent contractor. Any payments to him or her of $600 or more in a calendar year (excluding any housing allowance properly designated in advance by the board, TSA contributions, or reimbursed expenses) would require the issuing of a Form 1099-MISC and transmittal Form 1096 (Pensions n.d., Memo 1).

Your classification of individuals as either employee or self-employed should take place before any checks are written rather than at the end of the year when doing the W-2s and 1099s.

❊ Employees (Other than Clergy)

Typically, most of the workers that churches hire fall into this category. This can include associates in ministry, secretaries, office staff, organists, choir directors, and janitors. In very few instances do these individuals meet the requirements for being considered self-employed.

With the exception of unemployment benefits and some tax-deferred savings plans, for tax purposes workers of tax-exempt organizations such as churches are treated basically the same as workers of any other business. This means that the church is required to withhold the correct amounts of federal income tax, any applicable state tax, and social security tax from the employees' wages. The church also needs to match the amount of social security tax from its own funds. IRS *Circular E* (see enclosed CD for a copy of Publication 15, *Circular E—Employer's Tax Guide*) states that once an employee reaches $100 in wages, he or she is subject to FICA (social security) withholding. The church as the employer is required to make timely deposits of these taxes, file Form 941 every quarter, and at year-end issue a W-2 to each employee as well as a W-3 transmittal statement to the IRS along with copies of the W-2s.

Clergy

By far one of the most difficult concepts to understand is the employment status of the ordained clergy. Ordained ministers have "dual status treatment" under the provisions of the Internal Revenue Service code.

Payroll, Employees, and Ministerial Compensation

1. Ordained and full-time district-licensed ministers may generally be treated as employees for income tax purposes *(Revenue Ruling 80-110)*. But the IRS code exempts the ordained minister from federal income tax withholding (code section 3401 [a]).
2. Ordained and full-time district-licensed ministers are to be treated as self-employed for *social security reporting purposes.* However, while some clergy consider themselves self-employed, IRS Publication 517 states that in most cases ordained clergy are considered to be *employees* of the congregation. Page 1 reads as follows:

   > Even though you are considered a self-employed individual in performing your ministerial services for social security tax purposes, you may be considered an employee for income tax or retirement plan purposes. . . . some of your income may be considered self-employment income and other income may be considered wages.
   >
   > Common-law employee. Under the common-law rules, you are considered either an employee or a self-employed person depending on all the facts and circumstances. Generally, you are an employee if your employer has the legal right to control both what you do and how you do it, even if you have considerable discretion and freedom of action. . . .
   >
   > **Example.** A church hires and pays you a salary to perform ministerial services subject to its control. Under common-law rules, you are an employee of the church while performing those services.

A few other factors strongly suggest that pastors are indeed employees of the congregation.
- Employer-paid pension benefits
- Employer-paid medical benefits
- Workers' compensation insurance coverage

The benefits listed above are some typical employee benefits, but such things would never be given to a self-employed contract laborer. If your pastors are receiving the above benefits, the IRS would in most cases label them employees and advise that they should be getting W-2s at the end of the calendar year (Evangelical Lutheran 2007, chapter 9).

The consequences of classifying as an independent contractor someone who is actually an employee could include the assessment of federal withholding that should have been made, both halves of the FICA tax, inadvertently leaving the employee off the workers' compensation policy, and not considering the implications of the Fair Labor Standards Act for the employee.

💡 **Many church treasurers, before they give a check to anyone for services rendered, ask that the individual fill out a W-4. While the amount of the check issued may not exceed the IRS's mandated amount that requires a W-4 be submitted, the treasurer may find at the end of the year that additional payments to the individual have exceeded the maximum amount and a W-4 is indeed required. It is much easier for the treasurer to simply have everyone who receives a check fill out a W-4 from the first payment. This prevents time-consuming backtracking at the end of the year when the treasurer is preparing the church's taxes.**

What If We Do Not Withhold and Report?

There are criminal and civil penalties for willful failure to comply with requirements for withholding and reporting! In addition, the amount of certain taxes not withheld at the time of payment from an employee's salary (that must later be paid) becomes the responsibility of the employer! The employee has no obligation to later reimburse the employer for such amount. Further, in some cases, an officer or responsible employee may become personally liable for the taxes and penalties involved. That's right—the treasurer could be named as a defendant and held personally liable in a suit against the church.

Payroll, Employees, and Ministerial Compensation

The IRS has noted, for special review, tax returns of individuals reporting a significant proportion of income on Form 1099 from one source. Many such individuals are being reclassified as employees rather than independent contractors. This has resulted in additional cost, including penalties, for both the individual and the now determined employer. It is best to make the proper determination prior to such a review by the IRS (Pensions n.d., Memo 2).

What If We Are Not Sure Which Employment Relationship Exists?

The local church should carefully consult IRS Publication 15, *Circular E—Employer's Tax Guide,* and IRS Publication 15-A, *Employer's Supplemental Tax Guide* (both on enclosed CD), for examples that might be similar to the church's situation. Both forms are also available from the IRS by calling 1-800-TAX-FORM. Consultation should be made with a local legal and/or tax counselor for advice. If questions still arise, a special form is available from the IRS to request that they determine if such person has an employment relationship with the local church. In no case should the questions be ignored nor should there be willful failure to abide by legal requirements for withholding and reporting either wages paid to employees or payments in excess of $600 to unincorporated, independent contractors (Pensions n.d., Memo 2).

10 STEPS TO PREPARING FOR PAYROLL TAX OBLIGATIONS

Every congregation, as an employer, must report to the Internal Revenue Service with regard to the income paid to each employee. These 10 steps will prepare you to meet this obligation.

1. Acquire an Employer Identification Number (EIN). Every congregation should have one. If you happen to be a new congregation, then you must secure an EIN from the Internal Revenue Service. To obtain one, your congregation must complete Form SS-4, "Application for Employ-

er Identification Number," available from your local IRS office (a copy is included on the enclosed CD for your reference; please consult the "readme" file accompanying the IRS forms before using them). Once you are assigned a number, your congregation should automatically begin receiving:
- Form 941, "Employer's Quarterly Federal Tax Return"
- Form 8109, "Federal Tax Deposit Form"
- IRS Publication 15, *Circular E—Employer's Tax Guide*

2. Determine whether each worker is an employee or self-employed.
3. Have each *employee* complete a Form W-4. Have each *self-employed* individual complete a Form W-9. The Form W-4 for employees will give the congregation the necessary social security number, address of the employee, and the information required to withhold the correct amount of federal income tax. *Remember that any W-4 forms that claim more than 10 withholding allowances need to be reported to the IRS.* The Form W-9 for self-employed individuals will give the congregation the address and social security number of the individual. This information is needed when filing 1099s for these individuals at year-end. ❢ **If a self-employed worker performs services for your congregation and earns at least $600 for the year but fails to provide you with his or her social security number, then the congregation is required by law to withhold 28 percent of the amount of compensation as "backup withholding."**
4. Compute each employee's taxable wages. This, of course, means each employee's taxable wages also include the following:
    - Cash Christmas gifts from the congregation.
    - Social security offsets given to any clergy employees.
    - Imputed interest on low-interest (or no-interest) loans that the congregation might make to any employee.
    - Personal use of a church-owned vehicle.
    - Any business expense reimbursement given under a

nonaccountable business expense reimbursement arrangement. For example: a car allowance is given to an employee every month, but the congregation requires no recordkeeping or accounting for how the car allowance was spent. The total given as car allowance is considered taxable wage and at year-end would be included on the W-2. (See chapter 3, "Taxes," for more information on "accountable reimbursements.")

- Bonuses or any cash gifts.
- Forgiven debts.
- Most reimbursements of a spouse's travel expenses.

5. Determine the amount of income tax to withhold. IRS Publication 15 *(Circular E)* gives you two ways to calculate the correct amount of income tax to withhold. One way is called the wage bracket method in which you use the withholding tables in Publication 15. The other way is the percentage method in which the number of allowances claimed by the employee are multiplied by an appropriate value given in Publication 15.

   Normally federal income taxes are withheld only on the wages of the nonclergy. Clergy are exempt from withholding. A clergyperson can, however, ask to have federal income taxes withheld (but not FICA). To do this a clergyperson needs to fill out the W-4, giving a certain dollar amount that he or she would like to have withheld.

6. Withhold FICA taxes from nonclergy employees' wages. Congregations must withhold 7.65 percent of each employee's wage and also match this amount with their own funds. This 7.65 percent rate is composed of two items: (1) a Medicare hospital insurance tax of 1.45 percent on all taxable wages and (2) an "old-age, survivor and disability" tax of 6.2 percent—refer to your current year's tax guide to determine what the maximum taxable wage is for this category.

7. The congregation must deposit the taxes it withholds. As pointed out above, there are three components of federal

payroll taxes: (1) federal income taxes withheld from the employees' wages, (2) the employees' share of FICA taxes, and (3) the employer's share of FICA taxes. These dollars must be deposited according to the deposit status that the IRS determines for each congregation. In November of each year the IRS notifies all employers of their deposit statuses for the next year. The different rules are as follows:

- If withheld taxes are less than $500 at the end of any calendar quarter, the congregation need not deposit the taxes but rather may send them directly to the IRS with each quarterly Form 941.
- If withheld taxes were $50,000 or less during the most recent look-back period, the taxes are deposited monthly—by the 15th day of the following month.
- If withheld taxes were more than $50,000 during the most recent look-back period, the taxes are deposited semiweekly. This means that for paydays falling on Wednesday, Thursday, or Friday, the payroll taxes must be deposited on or by the following Wednesday. For paydays on Monday or Tuesday the taxes must be deposited on the Friday following the payday.
- Withheld taxes of $100,000 or more must be deposited by the next banking day.

Use Form 8109—"Federal Tax Deposit Coupon"—to deposit all employment taxes. The deposit can be made at any financial institution qualified to act as a depository for federal taxes or directly to the Federal Reserve bank serving your area. (If you are a new church just getting your EIN [employer identification number], five to six weeks after receiving your number the IRS will send you a booklet of tax deposit coupons, which are Forms 8109. [See IRS Publication 15 on the accompanying CD for more information.])

8. All employees subject to income tax withholding, social security taxes, or both must file Form 941 each quarter.

Payroll, Employees, and Ministerial Compensation

The 941 reports the amount of FICA taxes and the withheld income taxes that are payable. This total amount of tax should, of course, agree with the amount deposited or accumulated for that particular quarter. The Form 941 is due by the last day of the month following the end of each calendar quarter.

9. Prepare a W-2 form for each employee as well as the accompanying W-3 transmittal form for the IRS. The W-2s are due to employees by January 31; the W-3 by February 28.

Box *a*. No need to put anything here

Box *b*. Congregation's employer identification number

Box *c*. Congregation's name and address

Box *d*. Employee's social security number

Box *e*. Employee's name

Box *f*. Employee's address

Box 1. All wages earned by the employee for the year. Please see item 4 above for a discussion of what is considered taxable wage. Do not include that amount designated as housing allowance.

Box 2. The federal income tax withheld from that employee's wages. For most clergy this box can be left blank.

Box 3. The employee's wages subject to social security. Often this is the same amount as listed in Box 1 but not always, as some retirement contributions are excluded from Box 1 but included in Box 3. Box 3 should not list more than the maximum wage base for social security. For clergy employees, leave this box blank, as they are not subject to social security.

Box 4. Report the social security taxes withheld (6.2 percent of Box 3). Leave this blank for clergy employees.

Box 5. Report the employee's wages subject to Medicare. In most cases this will be the same as Box 3 except there is no maximum wage base for Medicare. Again, for clergy employees leave this box blank.

Box 6. Report the Medicare taxes withheld (1.45 percent of Box 5). Leave this blank for clergy employees.

Box 12. Insert the appropriate code and dollar amount in this box. Some of the codes that churches might use would be, for example, "C"—for providing more than $50,000 in group-term life insurance; "E"—for contributions made to a 403(b) tax-sheltered annuity through a salary reduction agreement; "L"—for the amount the church paid that equals the allowable standard mileage rate in the event the church paid at a rate higher than the IRS allowable rate. Any excess should be included in Boxes 1 and 3; "P"—the church reimbursed the employee's moving expenses, and the reimbursements are not included in the employee's income.

10. Prepare a 1099-MISC for each self-employed worker who earned $600 or more as well as the accompanying 1096 transmittal form for the IRS. The 1099s are due out by January 31, and the 1096 by February 28. To complete the 1099, note the following instructions:

Box 1. Report in this box the amounts paid to recipients for all types of "rents, such as equipment rentals, machine rentals, or office space rent."

Box 4. Report in this box any backup withholding.

Box 7. Report in this box the amount of compensation paid to the nonemployee (Evangelical Lutheran 2007, chapter 11).

MINISTERIAL COMPENSATION

A review of the patterns of ministerial compensation over several decades would indicate that significant changes have taken

Payroll, Employees, and Ministerial Compensation

place. Because of many social changes, gone are the days when the majority of ministers received a large portion of their compensation in the form of food and clothing supplied by members of the congregation. Today standard forms of ministerial compensation often include, but are not limited to, a cash salary, housing expenses (either an actual home or an allowance to pay for housing), FICA taxes, utilities, insurance (including health, life, and disability), some sort of retirement plan (many denominations sponsor retirement plans for pastors in which local churches can participate), and workers' compensation insurance.

The implications of the 1986 Tax Reform Act and subsequent IRS regulations also are among the reasons for these changes.

The 1986 Tax Reform Act had one of the most significant impacts on tax law since its previous major overhaul in 1954. Along with many other things for which it is blamed, the Act's revisions made it much more difficult for ministers to avoid paying income taxes on unreimbursed business expenses. For example, unreimbursed automobile expenses cannot be deducted dollar for dollar from compensation but must be deducted as a part of itemized deductions on Schedule A. With a high standard-deduction allowance, many parsonage families find it impossible to itemize deductions. The result is the payment of more income tax for those ministers who cannot deduct unreimbursed automobile expenses.

> Unreimbursed automobile expenses cannot be deducted dollar for dollar from compensation but must be deducted as a part of itemized deductions on Schedule A. With a high standard-deduction allowance, many parsonage families find it impossible to itemize deductions. The result is the payment of more income tax for those ministers who cannot deduct unreimbursed automobile expenses.

The same problem applies to many of the business and professional expenses a minister incurs in the exercise of ministry. In addition to the high standard-deduction allowance, these expenses must also exceed 2 percent of the adjusted gross income reported on the federal tax return. Furthermore, entertainment expenses are only 50 percent deductible if not reimbursed.

Such regulations have caused many ministers to reevaluate their compensation structuring.

IRS Regulations for Business Expense Reimbursements

Requirements for business expense reimbursements are based on IRS Regulation 1.62-2*(d)*(3). These requirements apply to every church and affect *all* employees. They are not optional—*they must be followed,* or the church employee may pay significantly greater amounts of *unnecessary* taxes.

> **The IRS regulations require that business reimbursements be included on Form W-2 as taxable income to the individual unless paid through an "accountable reimbursement plan" that has been "formally" adopted by the church board.**

The IRS regulations require that business reimbursements be included on Form W-2 as taxable income to the individual *unless* paid through an **"accountable reimbursement plan"** that has been "formally" adopted by the church board. The requirements for the accountable reimbursement plan are threefold: (1) The church may reimburse only those business expenses that an employee substantiates within 60 days of the expenditure with receipts and/or in writing as to the date, amount, place, and business nature. (2) The employee must return any "excess" reimbursements (i.e., unused expense advances) within 120 days of the expenditure. The excess reimbursement may not be treated as a bonus or gift. (3) Any advance must be made within 30 days of when the expense is paid or incurred.

Form W-2 income cannot simply be reduced "after-the-fact." In other words, the IRS will not allow the reimbursements to be paid through a retroactive reduction of salary. In order for reimbursements to be paid and qualify under an accountable reimbursement plan, properly substantiated expense reimbursements must be paid separately from the employee's salary. The salary amount and the accountable reimbursement plan must be established in advance of payment. If the church establishes a dollar limit on the expense plan (instead of reimbursing 100 percent of expenses), any balance remaining in the expense plan at year-end should remain with the church. If the balance is paid to the employee, all other plan payments made to the employee during the year become reportable as taxable income on Form W-2 (Pensions n.d., Memo 14).

Perhaps the easiest way to make a minister's expenses work under the accountable expense reimbursement plan is to give him or her a cash advance at the beginning of every month. During the month the pastor uses the advance for approved expenses and keeps all receipts for the costs. At the end of the month the pastor returns to the treasurer whatever cash is left from the advance and includes receipts and documentation for the balance.

Using this method the treasurer has some control over and knowledge of what expenses the minister has, and is receiving regular documentation for the IRS. The pastor benefits from this method in that the pastor's expenses are not taxed as part of his or her compensation, yet he or she still receives funds to pay for his or her expenses. (For more information on accountable reimbursement plans, see page 100 in chapter 3 and "Sample Accountable Expense Reimbursement Plan" in Appendix 2 and on acompanying CD.)

The Cost of a Minister vs. the Cost of a Ministry

For too long, churches and ministers have lumped together into a single concept the "cost of a minister" and the "cost of a ministry." These are actually two distinct concepts. For proper planning and church budgeting they must be kept separate.

The "cost of a ministry" includes those costs related to the work of the minister that are properly a part of local church expenses. Among these are the expenses that will be incurred without regard to which minister is serving the congregation at a particular time.

On the other hand, the "cost of a minister" relates to those items that are directly and indirectly related to compensating the particular pastor serving the church at the current time. These costs include the general categories of employee benefits and actual salary.

> The *least* advantageous way for a minister to be paid is to be given a lump sum amount out of which the minister must provide for professional expenses, employee benefits, and cash salary.

The *least* advantageous way for a minister to be paid is to be given a lump sum amount out of which the minister must provide for professional expenses, employee benefits, and cash salary. Unfortunately, in most situations where these are lumped together, both the local church and the minister assume that the total amount of the "package" is compensation. In reality, part is for the "cost of a ministry" and another part is for the "cost of a minister." See the chapter 3 "Accountable Reimbursement" section for more information.

What Is the Cost of a Ministry?

The following list includes business and professional expenses that are identified with the "cost of a ministry." They should be recognized and budgeted as local church expenses, not compensation.

When the minister is expected to pay for these items out of the amount provided in the church's "package," it will result in the parsonage family having to pay higher taxes on money they used to operate the local church's ministry. However, when these items are "reimbursed" through an accountable reimbursement plan (even if it means dividing the minister's previous "package" into two distinct amounts), it will usually result in lower taxes, a more accurate reflection of the minister's real compensation, and a simpler tax return to file.

The cost of maintaining ministry includes the following business and professional expense reimbursements:

- Automobile
- Continuing education

Payroll, Employees, and Ministerial Compensation

- Convention
- Hospitality
- Pastor's professional library
- Dues to professional organizations
- Church supplies (birthday cards, postage, etc.)
- Pastor's gifts "expected" to be given to members (wedding, baby, etc.)

What Is the Cost of a Minister?

The "cost of a minister" is made up of appropriate employee benefits, provisions for housing, and the actual cash salary paid.

Some of the items that are related to these are not discretionary, since the minister and family have no choice as to how the money is spent. The items of a nondiscretionary nature include most of the employee benefits listed below. The list includes the type of basic employee benefits that should be provided in a well-balanced compensation plan:

- Social security
- 403(b) retirement savings plan
- Health insurance
- Dental insurance
- Group term life insurance
- Long-term disability insurance
- Accidental death and dismemberment insurance
- Cash bonuses
- Paid holidays
- Vacation

The "cost of a minister" also includes the provision for housing: a cash housing allowance, a parsonage plus utilities, or a combination of the two. Most churches provide a parsonage and utilities. Thus in most cases the minister has no discretion as to how that part of compensation will be spent. The minister cannot voluntarily choose to live in a less expensive home and thereby free up income to cover other personal needs. Also, the minister

cannot build equity for retirement housing. The church board should recognize that when the minister leaves the church, a significant portion of the compensation that has been "paid" is left behind in the form of the parsonage. Fortunately, many churches are now recognizing their obligation to assist the minister in preparing for retirement housing by depositing monthly amounts into retirement savings plan accounts on a tax-advantaged basis.
❢ **If your church is not investing in a retirement account for your pastor and is unaware of what options exist, check with your denomination's pensions office or a tax adviser.** This is an essential part of the compensation package. See "Another Alternative" (page 70) for more information.

The remaining item in the "cost of a minister" is the cash salary. This is the amount that the minister and family use to meet living expenses and over which they have some discretion in spending. Among the factors that many church boards consider when determining their minister's cash salary are the following: the job requirements, the individual's professional qualifications, educational background, personal experience and expertise, the socioeconomic factors affecting the pay scale in the local community, and such subjective factors as merit pay for a job well done. Cost-of-living adjustments should be considered in each annual salary review of all church employees (Pensions n.d., Memo 14).

PARSONAGE OR HOUSING ALLOWANCE?

"Should we continue to provide a parsonage and utilities or should we change to a cash housing allowance and let our pastor buy his [her] own home?"

Many churches are asking this difficult question, often out of genuine concern for the pastor's dilemma at retirement, when he or she has no real estate investment built up for a retirement home. The question becomes even more difficult to answer with the shift in the nation's economy and in each local economic situation. While there is *no absolute, authoritative answer,* the follow-

Payroll, Employees, and Ministerial Compensation

ing list of advantages and disadvantages, which have become apparent to pastors and churches through actual experience, is offered to stimulate careful thinking and evaluation.

Pro Parsonage and Con Housing Allowance

1. In some situations there really is little choice. The parsonage may be connected to or adjoining the church building with no alternative for selling or renting. Unless used for Sunday School rooms, it remains the pastor's home.
2. Churches owning a parsonage may strengthen their ability to attract the pastoral candidate of their choice who may not be able or willing to buy a home.
3. In some areas there are no property taxes due on a church-owned parsonage, which may mean less expense is involved.
4. The church handles repairs and maintenance on the parsonage, thus freeing the minister from these time-consuming worries and expenses.
5. Often a parsonage is nicer than what a minister could afford to buy in the community.
6. Making a pastoral change is easier when moving from parsonage to parsonage, since securing temporary quarters is unnecessary for house hunting or waiting for occupancy.
7. When the parsonage is sold, the church loses a traditional and meaningful way of showing love and concern for the parsonage family.
8. Many ministers do not have sufficient funds for a down payment on a home.
9. The church that enters the loan business to "give" the pastor the down payment often bears the cost of low interest and little or no payment on the principal. There may be tax implications as well. State nonprofit corporation laws must be followed carefully. Some states may even prohibit such loans.
10. The loan situation is hopefully trouble free, but awkward situations have developed!

11. Many homes appropriate for the minister's needs are out of price range for his or her salary.
12. Very often the church cannot afford a housing allowance that fully covers all expenses, including real estate taxes, fire and casualty insurance, upkeep, and so on. It takes constant review and appropriate board action to keep pace with these increasing, inflationary costs.
13. Some pastors do not have the extra time, money, and expertise to handle such a real estate investment that includes the added responsibility of maintaining and repairing "his" or "her" home.
14. In some locations, real estate can move very slowly, if at all! Adequate housing may not be available for purchase when needed. Likewise, a home may not sell when it comes time for a pastoral change.
15. If the minister is the one who purchases the parsonage, any difference between purchase price and appraised value may be considered taxable as ordinary income.
16. Appreciation of property is assumed, but depreciation can be a reality due to natural and nonnatural disasters or economic conditions. Homeowners do not always sell at a profit. This potential is not a concern for the minister in a parsonage (Pensions n.d., Memo 1).

Pro Housing Allowance and Con Parsonage

1. A housing allowance may solve the problem of having to build a new parsonage at today's costs, while at the same time help the pastor plan for his or her retirement.
2. With a housing allowance, some feel that compensation planning may be more flexible, easier to compare, and simpler to budget.
3. Home ownership suggests permanency and may encourage longer pastorates.
4. Since a homeowner pays real estate taxes, he or she has more voice in community affairs.

5. A minister buying a home gets to choose the kind, style, and location.
6. The minister's family may decorate as they wish—even remodel without board action.
7. Home ownership becomes an important investment for the future, assuming, of course, each property appreciates in value and appropriate equity is established. This growing "earned equity" is portable as the minister relocates, allowing the minister to take his or her full earnings to a new location.
8. Home-owning ministers get a double tax break. Within certain limits, the housing allowance used to provide and furnish a home is nontaxable income. In addition, mortgage interest and property taxes are deductible as itemized deductions. (See chapter 3, "Taxes," for help determining who is a minister for tax purposes to see who qualifies for this double tax break.)
9. A homeowner can sell his or her principal residence and may not be required to pay any tax on up to *$500,000* of profit. The exclusion can be used as frequently as every two years. To be eligible, the homeowner must have owned and occupied the home as a primary residence for at least two of the five years before the sale. (The IRS has specific regulations controlling how this may be done.)
10. In the event of disability, death, or retirement, home ownership with adequate insurance generally means an immediate move is unnecessary (Pensions n.d., Memo 1).

Tax Implications

In addition to the above considerations, the local church board should insist that the tax implications be explored thoroughly before any decision is made. The following examples represent possible concerns:

- Extra care should be taken when a parsonage is to be given to a minister or sold to him or her at a value below the fair market value. The church may contend this is a "gift" and is not compensation. However, it is likely this would be challenged, forcing the minister to pay taxes on the value of the "gift" or take the issue to a tax court.

- Where the church does make such a considerable "gift" to their minister without reporting it as compensation, the church may be jeopardizing or calling into question its tax-exempt status. In order to have such status, the assets of the corporation cannot accrue to the personal benefit of an individual other than as reportable compensation. Tax-exempt organizations also must be careful that they are not paying "unreasonable" compensation to employees.

- Another concern involves the sale or rental of the parsonage. The church can be subject to taxation when it receives "unrelated business income." This possible interpretation of the tax laws should be explored before a final decision is made.

Another Alternative

The above lists are not intended to be exhaustive. Hopefully, they will stimulate thinking in this complex area. Many statements are similar but have opposite impact when phrased from a different perspective.

Churches with strong financial resources may have no difficulty if they decide to sell their parsonages and provide a cash housing allowance. However, such a decision should be preceded by careful evaluation and in consultation with the church board, any district or denominational board of local church properties, the pastor, and a tax adviser.

The church's governing council that does not allow its minister to purchase his or her own home but does provide an adequate parsonage and an allowance for parsonage furniture, and so on, is still without an answer for their concern for the pastor's future retirement need. But there is another alternative if the original question is rephrased: "How can we provide the pastor with an adequate salary now and also an adequate retirement nest egg without selling the parsonage?"

This question can sometimes be answered much more easily if your church is part of a denomination. Local denominational churches may sometimes provide a *retirement housing reserve* for their pastor by contributing into the denomination's tax-sheltered annuity or retirement plans. Check with your denominational pensions office or a tax adviser for a list of options that may be available to you (Pensions n.d., Memo 1).

OK. We've Decided on the Housing Allowance

One of the few significant tax advantages left for clergy is the ability to exclude from federally taxable income the rental value of a parsonage or that part of compensation that is used to provide a home (Internal Revenue Code section 107).

Section 107 consists of only one sentence, which currently states, "In the case of a minister of the gospel, gross income does not include—(1) the rental value of a home furnished to him as part of his compensation; or (2) the rental allowance paid to him as a part of his compensation, to the extent used by him to rent or provide a home and to the extent such allowance does not exceed the fair rental value of the home, including furnishings and appurtenances such as a garage, plus the cost of utilities."

Who Qualifies for the Housing Allowance?

- The individual must be employed by the church (or agency of the church).
- The individual must be ordained, commissioned, or licensed.
- The individual administers the sacraments.
- The individual conducts religious worship.
- The individual has management responsibilities in the church or denomination.
- The individual is considered to be a religious leader.

- The benefit is made available to the minister as compensation for services.

All of these need not apply. You will want to see the section in this chapter titled "Contractors, Employees, and Ministers" to discover further details regarding eligibility.

Tax regulations limit the housing allowance exclusion to the amounts paid for the home provided "as remuneration for services which are ordinarily the duties of a minister of the gospel" (Pensions n.d., Memo 13).

Bivocational ministers can have a housing allowance but only from their ministerial income. Generally, secular employers cannot give an employee a tax-free housing allowance, even if the employee is a minister.

What Kind of Expenses Can Be Used When Calculating the Housing Allowance Exclusion?

Generally, any expense to provide or maintain the home can be used to justify the housing exclusion. Regulations do specifically state that expenses for groceries, paper products, personal toiletries, personal clothing, and maid service cannot be used. You may legitimately include the following:
- Mortgage or rent payments
- Real estate taxes and interest
- Property insurance
- Down payment on a home
- Utilities
- Furnishings and appliances (purchase and repair of dishes, cookware; decorating items, including rugs, pictures, curtains, bedspreads, sheets, towels, etc.)
- Miscellaneous expenses, including improvements, repairs and upkeep of the home and its contents, snow removal, lawn mowing, lightbulbs, cleaning supplies, and so on.

No advance designation of housing values is required where the minister lives in a church-provided parsonage. This is also generally held to be true where the church has a stated policy of paying 100 percent of the parsonage utilities. The very act of paying the full amount is designation. However, ministers living in church-provided parsonages may have part of their cash compensation designated as a tax-free housing allowance to cover the cost of furniture purchase and repair, as well as other expenses related to the maintenance of the home that are not reimbursed by the church employer. Such an amount must be *designated in advance* as discussed below (Evangelical Lutheran 2007, chapter 10).

How Much of the Pastor's Salary Can Be Used as the Housing Exclusion?

The tax code contains no specific percentage or dollar limitation as to how much can be designated as housing allowance. A reasonable designation may be up to 100 percent of the cash compensation. However, it should be noted that a minister's cash housing allowance cannot exceed "reasonable compensation." This would apply only where a minister was performing very little service for the church and was receiving compensation disproportionate to the amount of service provided.

Only the lowest of the following amounts can be excluded for income tax purposes when the pastor files his or her federal income tax return:

- The fair rental value of the home, furnished plus utilities
- The amount actually used to provide a home
- The amount officially designated as the housing allowance

How Is the Difference Between the Designated Housing Allowance and the Lower of the Three Amounts Handled?

As indicated above, up to 100 percent of compensation can be "designated" as housing allowance, but this does not necessarily mean that this is the amount that can be excluded from income taxes. IRS Publication 517 provides a definition of how much parsonage allowance can be excluded for ministers. But essentially

- If the allowance exceeds the lower of the actual expenditures or the fair rental value, the pastor needs to include the difference on Form 1040 as "other income."
- If the actual expenditures or fair rental value exceed the allowance, the difference cannot be taken as an additional deduction on the pastor's tax return. It is lost.

The liability for determining the appropriate amount of housing allowance that can be excluded is the minister's. The church has no responsibility beyond determining that the compensation is reasonable for the services performed. The minister is responsible to determine any excess designated housing allowance and to report that amount as taxable income on the annual tax return.

When ministers pay off their mortgages, they can still have a housing allowance, but it cannot exceed the actual cost of maintaining the home. Some ministers who have paid off their homes try to include the "fair rental value" of their homes as housing allowance. This practice is not legal.

How Is the Housing Allowance Declared?

Tax regulations specify that for the housing allowance to be excluded from federal income taxes, it must be designated in advance of payment by official action of the employing church or integral agency.

- It should be adopted by the church board or congregation.
- It should be in writing.
- It should be in advance of the calendar year or in advance of a new pastor starting employment. (If a congregation fails to designate an allowance in advance of a calendar year, it should do so as soon as possible in the new year. The allowance will operate prospectively, never retroactively.)

The designation does not need to be attached to the tax return or reported to the IRS except upon specific inquiry.

It is recommended that the wording of the resolution be "open ended" so that the designation would be effective from that point forward until it is revised by the church board. Suggested resolutions follow:

- For a minister in a church-provided parsonage:
"Compensation for Rev. _____ will include a church-provided parsonage and the actual cost of utility expenses. For the purpose of covering additional housing-related expenses, $_____ per year is designated as housing allowance. This designation shall be effective until modified by the church board."
- For a minister purchasing his or her home or renting:
"The compensation for Rev. _____ shall include $_____ per year designated as housing allowance. This designation shall be effective until modified by the church board."
- For an evangelist:
"Compensation for Rev. _____, as evangelist, will include $_____ designated as housing allowance."

How Is the Housing Allowance Handled on the W-2?

The housing allowance (or the value of living in a church-owned parsonage) is always excluded from federal income. This means the congregational treasurer excludes this value from Box 1 of the W-2. Although there is no requirement to do so, the church can report this amount in Box 14 of the W-2, which is merely an information box (Evangelical Lutheran 2007, chapter 10).

Qualifying payments for a housing allowance are excluded from federal income tax. (However, these amounts are included in the computation of social security/Medicare taxes [SECA] at the self-employment tax rate.) Generally, housing allowance payments are also exempt from state income tax.

The minister's Form W-2 should not include any portion of the church-designated housing allowance. (See the "Form W-2" section of chapter 3, "Taxes," in this book for more information.) Housing expense details, receipts, and records should not to be submitted to the employer. They are handled different from professional business expenses and remain confidential. It is the individual minister's obligation to determine how much of the designation can actually be excluded and to report any unused portion of the designated amount as additional taxable income on the annual tax return.

It is recommended that the church treasurer provide a separate written notice at year's end to the minister indicating how much has been paid as designated cash housing allowance. This will be useful to the minister when he computes his or her social security/Medicare taxes (SECA) at the self-employment tax rate. A copy of the notification should be maintained in the church's file.

The proper designation of a cash housing allowance can result in significant tax savings for the qualifying minister. Here are the recommended steps for the minister to take in order to maximize the exclusion:

1. If in a parsonage with utilities paid in full, estimate the anticipated expense to maintain the home above what is provided by the church. Remember, this amount will need to meet the guidelines as outlined in IRS Publication 517.
2. If no parsonage is provided, compute the fair market rental value of your home plus utilities. You can include any fair market rental value of your furnishings.
3. Request the church to designate the amount determined in 1a or 1b above as housing allowance.
4. Maintain accurate records of appropriate expenses throughout the year to justify the housing allowance exclusion.
5. At the end of the tax year, determine if the housing allowance designated has been spent for the appropriate expenses. If not, then the difference between the amount designated and the amount spent must be included as additional taxable income when you fill out your federal income tax forms. Of course, this assumes the excluded amount does not exceed the "fair rental value," as discussed above (Pensions n.d., Memo 13).

Payroll, Employees, and Ministerial Compensation

CONFLICT OVER COMPENSATION ISSUES

One of the biggest causes of friction in the church often occurs between the pastor and the church treasurer. There are many reasons for this, but one reason includes this issue of pastoral compensation. As mentioned in both the chapter on taxes and this chapter on payroll, there are several things the local church can legally and ethically do to minimize the tax burden on the pastor. In some cases church treasurers and church-governing committees are not aware of such options, and being afraid of making a mistake that will cost the church in IRS penalties, they do nothing. Pastors have a right to be frustrated with this lack of support from their churches.

On the other hand, church treasurers often stay at the local church longer than the pastors and may have gone through the headaches of changing the pastor's overall compensation many times. It's hard to blame the treasurer of a church that seems to have had a revolving door for pastors when he or she becomes inflexible at adjusting the pastor's overall compensation package every two years and is accountable for tracking all taxable implications of the changes.

To help avoid some of this friction, the church's governing board should set up a written plan detailing all items of the pastor's compensation in summary form. We have included a sample form you can fill out and give to your pastor on a periodic basis (see Appendix 2 and CD form "Agreement of Understanding").

In addition to filling out an agreement of understanding with your pastor as to what his or her compensation will be, it is also good to track all the pastor's benefit expenses on a separate spreadsheet or ledger page. See chapter 4, "Budgeting, Reporting, and Financial Audits," for more on that topic.

Notice: This federal tax information is only a guide to help local churches with the legal requirements of being an employer. It is intended to provide some resources for further investigation. No attempt has been made to cover state and local income taxes or workers' compensation that would differ for each local church. Federal unemployment tax is not discussed either. Churches are generally exempt from this tax.

3
TAXES*

▶ Easily the most time-consuming and confusing part of the local church treasurer's job is the tracking of all expenditures for tax purposes. Knowing what to report, how to report it, and when to report it requires knowledge of many rules and regulations. While the treasurer does not need to commit all these regulations to memory, it is important for him or her to know where to find the information when needed.

The CD included with this book has copies of all the tax forms mentioned on these pages. However, tax forms change often. The forms included here are for reference only, and if not already outdated, they soon will be. Always be sure to get the most recent forms from your local post office, by calling 1-800-TAX-FORM, or by downloading them from the official Web site of the IRS at www.irs.gov. Also be sure to check www.beaconhillbooks.com for potential downloads, including updates to this packet and/or links to helpful sites. Note that many of the forms requiring reporting of wages are specially printed to be machine readable. Electronic copies of these particular forms from a personal computer are not acceptable for submission to the IRS.

Also note that although tax forms change, the numbers for each form do not. As you use the forms on the enclosed CD to collect the necessary information, you may be certain that requesting the updated form of the same number will ensure you receive the correct item.

---

*Special thanks to Pensions and Benefits USA for their excellent work that comprises a great deal of this chapter. Due to the continual changes that occur in the United States tax code, part of Pensions' ministry is to keep church treasurers apprised of the most recent changes that affect churches. For updates to the material presented in this chapter, visit the Pensions and Benefits Web site at pensions.nazarene.org.

TAX AND REPORTING PROCEDURES FOR CONGREGATIONS

The tax and reporting requirements with which churches must comply often seem to complicate the task of the local church treasurer. Many treasurers, who volunteer their services to the church, feel the special tax treatment of ministers adds another level of complexity to an already time-consuming task. This chapter is an overview of many of the basic federal tax and reporting issues.

CLASSIFICATION OF EMPLOYEES

Since legal and tax obligations of the church board as employer differ for the lay and ministerial employees, it is very important that the classification of each of its employees be determined accurately. The church may have employees who are considered by the church board to be performing ministerial duties but who are actually lay employees by IRS definitions.

Most churches will have at least one employee, the pastor. This is usually a *ministerial employee,* since most pastors either are ordained or district-licensed ministers. If a pastor holds *only* a limited "local" minister's license, this person's tax status with the IRS is that of a lay employee. Staff associates who are ordained or district-licensed ministers are generally ministerial employees *as long as they are performing ministerial functions* as outlined below. Other employees (e.g., secretaries and janitors) are *lay employees* even if ordained or district-licensed ministers.

The following classification summary may be helpful:

- **Self-employed**
    Itinerant evangelists and song evangelists who are *not* incorporated

- **Employees**
    Ministerial
    ▶ Pastor *who is an ordained* or district-licensed minister

▶ Staff member *who is an ordained* minister *and* who is performing ministerial or administrative duties (including deacons)

Lay

▶ Pastor who is not ordained or district-licensed, even if holding a *local* minister's license
▶ Church secretaries and church janitors
▶ Staff members who are *not* ordained or district-licensed ministers.
▶ Ordained or district-licensed ministers who are *not* serving in a ministerial or administrative capacity

These distinctions may not be consistent with the way the role of the individual is seen in the local church. However, they are important to understand because they are based on the IRS guidelines.

How the Courts Have Ruled

Court action in 1989 established five factors when determining whether one is a minister for tax purposes.

1. Does the individual administer the sacraments?
2. Does the individual conduct worship services?
3. Does the individual perform services in the "control, conduct, or maintenance of a religious organization" (Pensions n.d., Memo 12) under the authority of a church denomination or religious denomination?
4. Is the individual "ordained, commissioned, or licensed" (Pensions n.d., Memo 12)?
5. Is the individual considered a spiritual leader by his or her religious body?

Employees who meet some but not all of these factors may or may not be considered ministers. Under the 1989 tax court case, not all factors had to be satisfied. It should be noted that *only factor 4, that one be "ordained, commissioned, or licensed," needs to be present in every case.* The more of the remaining criteria that one can meet, the more likely one is to fulfill the definition of "minister of the gospel." (However, some more recent court cases and an IRS Private Letter Ruling have required that all factors be satisfied. Nevertheless, according to leading church law experts, the 1989 case is still a viable precedent. The income tax regulations noted previously remain the reliable source for determining ministerial qualification.) Also, the tax court *has not* recognized persons as ministers for tax purposes who were licensed solely to gain tax benefits. In other words, if one seeks a district license or ordination simply to gain tax benefits rather than the rights and privileges associated with it, then the IRS likely would not view that individual as a minister for tax purposes.

> **If one seeks a district license or ordination simply to gain tax benefits rather than the rights and privileges associated with it, then the IRS likely would not view that individual as a minister for tax purposes.**

THE MINISTERIAL EMPLOYEE

Each year, the church should issue Form W-2 to each of its employees, including all ministerial employees. However, the issuance of Form W-2 *does not* affect how a ministerial employee pays income tax and social security/Medicare tax (SECA) (using the self-employment tax rate) to the IRS.

A minister can make estimated quarterly tax payments to the IRS (Form 1040-ES). Or the minister and the local church may enter into a *voluntary* arrangement whereby the church withholds federal (and possibly state and local) income taxes. (The local church has *no obligation* to withhold federal income tax from the ministerial employee. However, each church will need to check the applicable rules regarding withholding state and local income taxes.)

If the church withholds income taxes under a voluntary arrangement, the income tax withheld must be remitted to the IRS on at least a quarterly basis. Quarterly payroll tax returns (Form 941) also must be filed. A thorough understanding of this process should be obtained before entering into a voluntary withholding agreement. Your local tax consultant can help.

Today many churches "pay" to their ministers a social security/Medicare tax "allowance." This "allowance" for the minister's SECA tax liability must be reported as taxable income on Form W-2 (Box 1). Furthermore, it is also taxable for social security (SECA) purposes when the ministerial employee files Schedule SE with the yearly income tax return (Pensions n.d., Memo 2).

THE LAY EMPLOYEE

Upon hiring a lay employee, the church becomes obligated to withhold federal (and state and local as applicable) income tax and social security/Medicare tax (FICA) from the employee's salary and to report that salary and withholding to the IRS and to the individual. Failure to withhold and report can result in penalties and serious problems that should be carefully avoided. For example, in a federal court ruling, four church officers each were held personally responsible for over $200,000 of the church's unpaid payroll taxes. Obligations, procedures, and tables for withholding federal income tax and social security/Medicare tax (FICA) are in IRS Publication 15, *Circular E—Employer's Tax Guide* (available on the enclosed CD or from the IRS by calling 1-800-TAX-FORM).

All lay employees (both full-time and part-time) are automatically covered by social security/Medicare under the FICA plan. This requires withholding one-half of the taxes from the employee, paying a matching amount from the employer's own funds, remitting the funds to the proper depository institution, and reporting this total to the IRS on Form 941 each quarter.

THE EMPLOYER IDENTIFICATION NUMBER

Your congregation is required to report employment taxes (federal income taxes and social security/Medicare taxes withheld) and give Form W-2 to employees, including the minister, whether or not any taxes are withheld. Thus your church should already have a federal Employer Identification Number (EIN) and in some states a state identification number. *Your congregation must use the EIN on all items sent to the IRS.*

If your church is new and does not have an EIN, IRS Form SS-4, used to request the federal Employer Identification Number, can be secured from the IRS by calling 1-800-TAX-FORM (a copy for your reference is on the enclosed CD). The absence of the appropriate identification number may cause unnecessary and improper reporting of any amounts withheld for income and/or social security/Medicare taxes. It might also cause unnecessary scrutiny of the employee's tax records for previous years. When the IRS supplies the EIN, they will provide a copy of *Circular E,* complete with instructions on withholding, remitting, and reporting federal employment taxes.

If your church has an EIN but is not receiving quarterly and annual payroll tax forms, simply call the IRS, provide them with your EIN, state that you now have a requirement to file tax returns, and ask them to provide you with a copy of *Circular E* and the necessary reporting forms.

WHAT IS TAXABLE FOR FEDERAL INCOME TAX PURPOSES?

For the ministerial employee, taxable income consists of

- cash salary paid as compensation
- any cash bonuses or "love offerings"
- automobile or other "allowances" (if not paid under an "accountable reimbursement plan" as described later in this chapter)
- social security/Medicare tax "allowances"
- taxable fringe benefits

Taxes

Taxable income *does not* include

- a housing allowance or the fair market rental value of a church-owned parsonage
- 403*(b)* retirement savings plan contributions
- business and professional expense reimbursements (e.g., business-related transportation/travel, meals, books, dues, office supplies, etc.), provided such reimbursements are paid under an "accountable reimbursement plan," as described later in this chapter
- any other tax-free benefits allowed by the IRS, such as health and dental insurance when premiums are paid or reimbursed by the church

Subject to certain housing allowance limitations, the greatest exclusion for the ministerial employee is the value of housing and utilities provided, or the cash compensation designated as housing allowance and used for that purpose (Pensions n.d., Memo 3).

For the lay employee, taxable income consists of

- cash salary paid as compensation
- any cash bonuses or "love offerings"
- automobile or other "allowances" (if not paid under an "accountable reimbursement plan")
- social security/Medicare tax "allowances"
- taxable fringe benefits
- housing allowance

It *does not* include

- 403*(b)* retirement savings plan contributions
- business and professional expense reimbursements (e.g., business-related transportation/travel, meals, books, dues, office supplies, etc.), provided such reimbursements are paid under an "accountable reimbursement plan"

- any other tax-free benefits allowed by the IRS, such as health and dental insurance when premiums are paid or reimbursed by the church

The *cash* housing allowance or the fair market rental value of a parsonage and utilities must be reported as taxable income for lay employees. Only ordained or district-licensed ministers performing ministerial or administrative duties may claim the housing exclusion provided by Section 107 of the Internal Revenue Code (Pensions n.d., Memo 13).

INCOME TAX WITHHOLDING

For the ministerial employee, federal (and possibly state and local) *income* tax may be withheld if the minister and the church enter into a voluntary arrangement. Otherwise, the ministerial employee generally will need to file and pay estimated tax (Form 1040-ES) to cover federal income tax and social security/Medicare tax (SECA) obligations. Even if a voluntary withholding arrangement is used, *FICA taxes should never be withheld from a minister.*

For the lay employee (both full-time and part-time), the employer *must* withhold income tax according to the provisions of the tax law. There are fines and penalties for failing to comply. The employer must secure Form W-4 on which the employee claims any exemptions for self and dependents. The amount withheld is then determined by using the charts provided by the IRS in Publication 15, *Circular E—Employer's Tax Guide.*

Care must be taken with lay employees to withhold on all taxable income, *including* the value of housing and utilities provided.

SOCIAL SECURITY/MEDICARE TAX WITHHOLDING

For the ministerial employee, the church *cannot* withhold for social security/Medicare (FICA) taxes as it does for lay employees. The law provides that payment be made directly by the ministerial employee as if self-employed. The tax is based on the current self-employment rates. This rate must be applied on taxable income (i.e., salary, cash bonuses or "love offerings," automobile or other "allowances," social security/Medicare tax "allowances," taxable fringe benefits) *and housing allowance* (whether a cash allowance or the fair market rental value of housing and utilities provided). Many churches provide to the minister a social security/Medicare tax allowance equal to the full amount. That allowance, in turn, becomes taxable for income and SECA tax purposes.

For the lay employee, social security laws state that *all* lay employees (both full-time and part-time) are covered automatically by social security/Medicare tax withholding rules under FICA. Thus all church employers *must* withhold FICA at the current employee rates from the lay employee's wages that are subject to social security/Medicare taxes (including any "salary-reduction" 403*[b]* retirement savings plan contributions) *and pay a matching amount from their own church funds.* The total is then paid to the government for the individual. Many churches may want to give an allowance to the lay employee equal to the full amount withheld. Of course, such an allowance becomes taxable income.

FORM W-4

All employees, whether part-time or full-time, should complete a Form W-4, "Employee's Withholding Allowance Certificate." That form reports the number of withholding allowances requested by the employee and is the basis upon which the amount of federal income tax to be withheld is determined. Generally, a Form W-4 remains valid until a new one is filled out or is required by the IRS. All W-4 forms are retained by the employer. (If any employee, other than the minister, reports no tax to be withheld or claims more than 10 withholding allowances, copies of those W-4 forms generally must be sent to the IRS by the employer.)

You should keep on file your minister's Form W-4, noting that no federal taxes are to be withheld pursuant to Section 3401*(a)*(9) of the Internal Revenue Code that specifically exempts a minister's wages from income tax withholding. Of course, *if* the minister and church have agreed to voluntary withholding of *income taxes* (not social security—FICA taxes), then the Form W-4 should indicate the correct number of withholding allowances and any amount of extra withholding requested.

Employees who had no income tax liability in the previous year and do not expect to pay a tax in the current year may request that no income taxes be withheld in the current year by completing the appropriate lines on Form W-4. (Note: some exceptions apply.)

On another line of Form W-4, employees *may* request that additional federal income tax be withheld. *If* your minister elects to have income taxes withheld *and* desires additional income tax to be withheld to cover the personal obligation of the social security/Medicare (SECA) tax payment (which must be paid at the self-employment rate), that amount should be shown on the proper line.

> Taxes deducted from the salary checks are to be segregated into separate accounts in the treasurer's bookkeeping system. There are very specific instructions on the frequency of depositing these funds.

DEPOSIT OF WITHHELD AMOUNTS

Taxes deducted from the salary checks are to be segregated into separate accounts in the treasurer's bookkeeping system. There are very specific instructions on the frequency of depositing these funds. IRS Publication 15, *Circular E—Employer's Tax Guide,* explains this process in detail. Deposits must be made properly and on a timely basis to avoid late penalties. Each quarter, Form 941 must be filed to report the amounts withheld to IRS.

Form 941

You should receive Form 941 automatically each quarter from the IRS. These forms are to be used to report the taxes your congregation has withheld and which are owed for each quarter. This form is used to report both federal income taxes and FICA taxes withheld.

Taxes

By the last day of the month, following the end of each quarter, Form 941 must be filed. There are penalties for not doing so. You may wish to file the form *even if* no taxes are withheld. Technically, there is no requirement to file when no taxes are withheld.

As soon as you owe more than $2,500 for employment taxes (withholding of federal income and FICA taxes, as well as the employer's FICA taxes), your congregation must pay that money by the method required by the IRS. You should automatically receive instructions for making those payments along with a supply of IRS computer-readable forms (unless you must use an electronic payment process). All federal employment taxes due must be paid at least quarterly, and more frequent deposits may be required.

Here are a *few* of the items you will report on Form 941:

1. On line 2, report the total of all wages paid and any other compensation paid by the employer, whether or not the employer is required to withhold federal income tax or social security tax. Thus this line includes the minister's salary.
2. On line 3, report the total federal income tax withheld from wages. (If you wish, you may indicate in the lower margin of the form the number of ministerial employees included on line 1 and their compensation you had to include on line 2 that is "not subject to withholding pursuant to IRC Section 3401*(a)*(9)" [Pensions n.d., Memo 3].)
3. On lines 6*a*, 6*b*, 7*a*, and 7*b*, report the appropriate totals for applicable FICA wages paid and Medicare wages paid (these may not be the same amounts as reported on line 2) and the amount of tax due on those wages (employee *and* employer taxes). Since your ministerial employees are not subject to FICA and Medicare withholdings, do not include their compensation in these totals.
4. On line 11, report total taxes. This will include withheld taxes and the taxes due from the employer for both FICA and Medicare.

You must also report on Form 941 (line 14) any *deposits* made for accumulated withholdings. A record of tax liability (not deposits) for each month of the quarter also is required (line 17). Upon filing Form 941, *any taxes still due must be paid.*

FORM W-2

If your congregation does not receive a supply of employment tax forms before the end of the year, you will want to request them by calling the IRS (1-800-TAX-FORM). By January 31, each employee must be given Form W-2 reporting wages paid during the preceding tax year.

The IRS, in Publication 517 (included on the enclosed CD), has indicated clearly for a number of years that the church employer should provide the *minister* with a Form W-2 at the end of the tax year. This is true even though there may have been no withholding for federal income tax due to the exemption and even though the minister's wages are not subject to withholding for social security/Medicare tax (FICA).

The *lay employee* must also receive Form W-2 from the church. Since the employer is required to withhold for federal income tax and any applicable social security/Medicare taxes, the treasurer can determine the amount withheld and the amount of taxable wages from the accounting records. Taxable wages must include the value of any housing or utilities provided.

Form W-2 requires the employer's name, address, zip code, and Employer Identification Number (EIN), as well as the employee's name, address, zip code, and social security number.

- In Box 1, show wages paid.
- In Box 2, show any federal income tax withheld.
- Boxes 3, 4, 5, and 6 are completed with dollar amounts *only* for lay employees. (For ministers, Boxes 3, 4, 5, and 6 should be left blank.)

The following statements give general guidelines that apply to the minister's Form W-2 and the lay employee's Form W-2. Spe-

Taxes

cific instructions can be secured from any local IRS office or by calling 1-800-TAX-FORM.

On the minister's Form W-2, report salary (cash and noncash) paid in Box 1. Include any social security allowance, automobile or other "allowances" (if not paid under an "accountable" reimbursement plan), taxable fringe benefits, and church-paid "love offerings." Exclude any automobile or other business reimbursements that have been paid through an accountable reimbursement plan, contributions to a 403*(b)* retirement savings plan, and any designated housing allowance. If federal income tax has been withheld from a minister's wages, fill in Box 2; otherwise leave it blank. Leave Boxes 3, 4, 5, and 6 blank.

On the lay employee's Form W-2, report salary (cash and noncash) paid in Box 1 just as you did for the minister but also include any housing allowance. (The *cash* housing allowance *or* the fair market rental *value* of a parsonage and utilities must be reported as taxable income for lay employees. Only ordained or district-licensed ministers serving in a ministerial capacity can exclude it from income taxes.) Automobile and other business reimbursements paid through an accountable reimbursement plan are excluded from Boxes 1, 3, and 5. All 403*(b)* retirement savings plan contributions are excluded from Box 1; however, only employer-paid contributions over and above salary are excluded from social security/Medicare wages, Boxes 3 and 5. Voluntary salary reduction 403*(b)* contributions are included in Boxes 3 and 5, and tax withheld must be reported on these funds, Boxes 4 and 6.

Box 12—*Follow the Form W-2 instructions carefully.* Any entry made should be carefully entered and labeled according to IRS codes provided in your Form W-2 instructions to avoid confusion in reporting these amounts. If more than four items need to be reported in Box 12, use a separate Form W-2. The following items may need to be considered when completing Box 12.

- **Group Term Life Insurance.** If the church employer pays for more than an aggregate of $50,000 of group-term life insurance for an employee, the cost of the coverage over $50,000 must be reported both in Box 12 using Code C and in Box 1 (also in Boxes 3 and 5 if a lay employee).

- **Deferred Compensation.** Any contributions made through the church to an employee's 403*(b)* retirement savings plan under a voluntary salary reduction agreement must be reported in Box 12 using Code E. This amount would not be included in Box 1 for either ministerial or lay employees. This amount would be included in Boxes 3 and 5 for a lay employee.

- **Moving Expenses.** Qualified moving expenses paid for or reimbursed to an employee do not represent taxable income. However, any *non*qualified moving expenses paid for or reimbursed to an employee represent taxable income reportable in Box 1 for ministers and in Boxes 1, 3, and 5 for lay employees (since these payments are subject to social security and Medicare tax for lay employees). Excludable moving expenses paid directly to an employee must be reflected in Box 12 using Code P. No Form W-2 reporting is required for employer payments of qualified moving expenses paid directly to a vendor for an employee.

Box 13—One item may apply to church employees. It is "Retirement Plan."

"Retirement Plan"—This item must be checked if the employee is an active participant (for any part of the calendar year) in a retirement plan maintained by the church employer.

All employees performing ministerial duties who are district-licensed ministers or ordained ministers and who have served as either pastors or as full-time associates earning their full livelihood from that ministry must have Box 13, "Retirement Plan," checked.

A lay employee having a 403*(b)* contribution *only* under a voluntary salary reduction basis would *not* have this item checked since it would already be indicated in Box 12 using Code E.

Taxes

Box 14—If the church owns or leases a vehicle for an employee's use, the value of the "personal and nonbusiness" use of that vehicle is taxable income. The value of the use of the vehicle is established by using official tables available from the IRS (1-800-TAX-FORM). The amount of the *personal and nonbusiness use* must be included in Box 1 and in Box 14 (and in Boxes 3 and 5 if a lay employee). The employee must maintain a mileage log or similar records to substantiate business and personal use of the vehicle and submit this to the employer. If not substantiated, the employer must report 100 percent of the use of the vehicle as taxable income.

If the employee fully reimburses the employer for the value of the personal use of the vehicle, then no value would be reported in either Box 1 or in Box 14. You may want to refer to IRS Publication 535 for more information on vehicle usage valuation and reporting.

FORM W-3

In order to transmit the W-2 forms to the IRS, your congregation must file Form W-3, "Transmittal of Wage and Tax Statements." Form W-3 will be provided to your congregation at year's end with the supply of employment forms from the IRS. A copy for your information is also included on the enclosed CD.

The purpose of Form W-3 is to summarize for the IRS the number of W-2 forms being transmitted. Information required includes the name, address, zip code, and EIN of the employer; the number of W-2 forms being transmitted; the total amount of wages, federal income taxes withheld, social security/Medicare (FICA) taxes withheld, and FICA wages reported on all of the W-2 forms. Totals on Form W-3 should balance to the aggregate of the totals reported on any 941 forms filed for the year.

Form W-3 and all attached W-2 forms must be submitted to the IRS by the last of February (unless that day falls on a weekend, then by the following Monday). No money is sent with the Form W-3.

FORM W-5

Form W-5, "Earned Income Credit Advance Payment Certificate" (EIC), is used by eligible employees ("low-income" employees) who elect to receive advance payments of the earned income credit. IRS Publication 15, *Circular E—Employer's Tax Guide,* describes the use of the EIC. If a minister is the only employee of the church and a voluntary withholding arrangement does not exist, the church is not liable for the EIC.

FORM 1099-MISC

While the church generally is not required to withhold taxes from nonemployees, Form 1099-MISC must be filed for payments to a self-employed person or *un*incorporated business if payments have been $600 or more per year. This includes payments to independent contractors and *un*incorporated evangelists (excluding any housing allowance properly designated in advance, 403*(b)* retirement savings plan contributions, or reimbursed expenses). Payment of attorney's fees must be reported even if the firm providing the legal services is incorporated. Transmit copies of Form 1099-MISC to the IRS with Form 1096.

RECORDS

Your congregation must keep accurate records of all wages paid and taxes withheld. Keep an individual ledger sheet or computer log for each employee plus a similar summary sheet for all wages paid to all employees.

SHORT CHECKLIST FOR TAX PROCEDURES

1. Employer requests Employer Identification Number (EIN) if not already assigned.
2. *All* employees should have a valid Form W-4 on file with the employer.
3. Employer withholds federal income taxes and any applica-

Taxes

ble social security/Medicare (FICA) taxes from *each* paycheck, *except* paychecks of the clergy in the exercise of ministry unless the clergy and church have entered a voluntary agreement for withholding federal income taxes.
4. Employer files Form 941 by the end of the month following each quarter and pays any balance due of taxes withheld.
5. At year's end, the employer issues a Form W-2 to *all employees* and files Form W-3 transmittal.
6. Employer issues Form 1099-MISC to whom necessary and files Form 1096 with the IRS.

CHECKLIST FOR FILLING OUT BOX 1 OF FORM W-2

Minister Only	Both	Layperson Only	—
—	Yes	—	Salary
No	—	Yes	Housing/furnishings allowance (designated in advance)
No	—	Yes	Parsonage rental value
No	—	Yes	Utilities paid by church
—	Yes	—	Social Security/Medicare "allowance"
—	No	—	Transportation/travel and other business and professional expense reimbursements only if paid under a board-adopted accountable reimbursement plan
—	Yes	—	"Reimbursements" if not paid under an accountable reimbursement plan

—	Yes	—	Church love offerings or cash gifts in excess of $25
—	No	—	Contributions to the 403(b) retirement savings plan
—	No	—	Health/dental insurance premiums paid or reimbursed by the church
—	No	—	Group term life insurance premiums (for up to $50,000 coverage) paid directly by the church
—	No	—	Moving expense reimbursements that do not exceed deductible moving expense

MINIMIZING INCOME TAXES FOR CHURCH EMPLOYEES

One of the many responsibilities that church boards face is that of minimizing income taxes for their church employees by appropriately structuring compensation packages. IRS tax rulings not only make this possible but also make it very important. *Unfortunately, some church employees pay additional income taxes simply because of the way their church employer has established their salary structures.* Changing IRS regulations and current rulings make it all the more important for church boards to periodically review the salary structures of all their employees.

This review is also important from the standpoint that IRS procedures require the church employer to issue annual wage and tax statements, Form W-2s, to *all* church employees, both lay and ministerial. The church treasurer's bookkeeping accounts should be set up to carefully reflect the amounts that should and should not be reported on the annual Form W-2s (Pensions n.d., Memo 3).

Tax-Free Employee Benefits

In addition to "cash" salary, an employee usually receives some benefits that are paid for by the employer. Many of these benefits are "tax-free" to the employee if paid directly by the employer (not reimbursed). Unfortunately, some church employees are paying for these "benefits" out of their pockets with after-tax dollars and are therefore losing a legitimate tax advantage simply because of the manner of payment. Some examples of employee benefits that may be provided by the employer for the employee on a tax-free basis include health insurance, dental insurance, group-term life insurance, some tax-sheltered annuity plans, salary continuance insurance, and accidental death and dismemberment insurance.

Business Transportation, Travel, and Related Expenses

Most church employees incur business transportation and travel expenses in the course of conducting the ministry of the local church. Many churches are careful to reimburse their employees *in full* for these expenses.

Often, church employees also incur business and professional expenses in their ministries. Examples include business-related entertainment, professional books and magazines, memberships and dues in professional organizations, stationery and supplies, and other ministry expenses. Normally, the church board recognizes these as necessary for the work of the church and views them as local church expenses. The employee should be reimbursed in full. If these expenses are paid properly through an *accountable reimbursement plan,* the IRS says they are not reportable as income.

For example, reimbursable phone expenses may include long-distance calls, a second line, special equipment, and services such as call waiting if there is a business relationship. Basic local service charges (including taxes) for the first line in the home are not considered a business expense.

Another example is entertainment expenses for church business. Only 50 percent of meals and entertainment as a business expense are deductible on Form 2106 (or Form 2106-EZ) and Schedule A. However, if the business meals and entertainment are presented to the church with proper documentation under an accountable reimbursement plan, then 100 percent may be reimbursed. This illustrates how important it is for every church employee to utilize an accountable reimbursement plan.

Likewise, qualifying educational expenses may be reimbursed *in full* under an accountable reimbursement plan. Typical expenses include tuition, books, supplies, transportation away from the employee's hometown, meals, lodging (if necessary to be away from home overnight to attend classes), and correspondence courses. Qualifying educational expenses are those incurred to meet the requirements of the employee's church to keep his or her present position or to maintain or improve skills in his or her present employment. Expenses do not qualify, even though these requirements are met, if the education is required for the employee to meet the minimum educational requirements of his or her occupation, or part of a program of study that will qualify the employee for a new occupation. For example, a minister who has not been gainfully employed as a minister will not be able to count his or her seminary education. However, a pastor who is obtaining additional education likely will qualify. An employee must not be absent from his or her profession for more than a year. The IRS considers it a career change if you work a secular job for more than a year while obtaining additional education. Also, travel costs claimed as a "form of education" (i.e., a trip to the Holy Land) do not qualify. However, enrollment in a formal course of study overseas may qualify.

❢ Probably the largest business expense for a minister is the auto expense. Some churches continue to provide a

nonaccountable "car allowance." However, the IRS says such nonaccountable "allowances" are to be reported as income on Form W-2.

In recognition of the fact that these are business expenses and not personal expenses, the IRS allows these reimbursements to be provided tax-free to the employee if they are paid through an accountable reimbursement plan. Unfortunately, sometimes reimbursements are insufficient to cover actual expenses. In such cases, employees find themselves paying out of their own salaries what is recognized as a local church operating expense. However, careful planning can ensure that your church employees' salaries are actually theirs to spend.

In the past, an employee used Form 2106 to deduct unreimbursed expenses from income taxes. However, the Tax Reform Act of 1986 changed the procedures for using Form 2106 to the extent that many employees may not be able to claim the deductions. This makes it even more important that all business transportation, travel, and related expenses be fully reimbursed. Full reimbursement for automobile mileage should be either on a dollar-for-dollar basis for business expenses incurred or on a cents per mile basis at the standard mileage rate. It is necessary to maintain accurate records of business mileage and/or expenses. However, instead of using the records to support a deduction on tax forms, they should be supplied to the church treasurer as substantiation for the reimbursements.

❡ If the reimbursements are paid properly through an accountable reimbursement plan, the IRS recognizes these reimbursements as tax free. When a church employee incurs this type of expense and is not reimbursed in full, the situation becomes a bit more complicated.

The ministerial or lay employee *may* be able to treat *a portion of* the *un*reimbursed business and professional expense (if proper substantiation is provided) as a tax *deduction.* As such, it would be claimed on Schedule A, "Itemized Deductions," when the annual tax return is filed. By using this means, some employees may be able to deduct *a portion of* their expenses, but many will lose the tax break. This is because in order to claim these items as deductions, the expenses must exceed 2 percent of adjusted gross income and the individual employee must file an itemized return and have more deductions than the standard deduction. If all itemized deductions do not exceed the standard deduction, the *un*reimbursed business and professional expenses will simply be absorbed and lost in the standard deduction amount. The Tax Act of 1993 limited the deductibility of many entertainment expenses to 50 percent of value. Thus 50 percent of these types of *un*reimbursed business expenses cannot be deducted even if all other conditions are met.

Whether the *un*reimbursed business expenses are taken as a tax deduction or are lost in the standard deduction amount for income tax purposes, there still remains the question of social security/Medicare taxes. Either way, the ministerial employee could avoid self-employment taxes (SECA—social security/Medicare taxes) on the total of *un*reimbursed business expenses, since many of those expenses remain exempt from SECA taxes. However, the lay employee would not be able to recover any FICA taxes withheld nor would the church be able to recover their portion of FICA taxes paid.

The Accountable Reimbursement Plan

Requirements for business expense reimbursements are based on IRS Regulation 1.62-2*(d)*(93). These requirements apply to *every* church and affect *all* employees. They are not optional— *they must be followed,* or the church employee may pay significantly greater amounts of *unnecessary* taxes.

The IRS regulations require that business reimbursements be included on Form W-2 as taxable income to the individual *unless* paid through an "accountable reimbursement plan" that has been "formally" adopted by the church board. The requirements for the accountable reimbursement plan are threefold: (1) The church may reimburse only those business expenses that an employee substantiates within 60 days of the expenditure with receipts and/or in writing as to the date, amount, place, and business nature. (2) The employee must return any "excess" reimbursements (i.e., unused expense advances) within 120 days of the expenditure. The excess reimbursement may not be treated as a bonus or gift. (3) Any advance must be made within 30 days of when the expense is paid or incurred.

Form W-2 income cannot simply be reduced "after-the-fact." In other words, the IRS will not allow the reimbursements to be paid through a retroactive reduction of salary. In order for reimbursements to be paid and qualify under an accountable reimbursement plan, properly substantiated expense reimbursements must be paid separately from the employee's salary. The salary amount and the accountable reimbursement plan must be established in advance of payment. If the church establishes a dollar limit on the expense plan (instead of reimbursing 100 percent of expenses), any balance remaining in the expense plan at year-end should remain with the church. The payment of the balance to the employee makes all payments made to the employee under the plan during the year reportable as taxable income on Form W-2.

What the Church Could Do

Obviously, most churches will want to make sure that church employees are fully reimbursed for *all* their business-related expenses through an accountable reimbursement plan, since the IRS recognizes these reimbursements as nontaxable to the employee for income tax and social security/Medicare tax purposes. When this is done, the employee's "salary" can remain whole. Since the auto expense is usually the largest business expense for ministers, churches should make sure this is on the list of accountable expense reimbursements. The church board or governing committee may decide to reimburse the minister for only actual costs, but the simplicity of using the standard mileage rate is compelling.

If a church finds that it simply cannot afford to reimburse all the business-related expenses that its employees are incurring, it can still attempt to minimize the income tax for the employee. The church board may wish to consider the following plan:

1. The church board will want to consider first how many of these expenses it can begin to fully reimburse now through a board-adopted accountable reimbursement plan. (It will also want to develop a plan whereby it can begin reimbursing any remaining expenses as soon as possible.)

2. The church board, in working with the church employee, will want to determine how much of the present salary is actually being spent for unreimbursed business-related expenses. Together they can then arrive at a new "salary" figure that truly reflects the actual cash compensation the church board is paying to the individual.

3. The difference between the two figures (i.e., the amount that is being paid out of personal salary for these unreimbursed expenses) should now be designated in the budget for the reimbursement of these expenses.

4. The newly determined actual salary to be paid weekly or monthly in regular amounts should be recognized in a separate action by the church board or governing committee. It would be reported on Form 941. The salary would not be adjusted "after-the-fact" to reflect local church expenses.

5. A portion of the business expense reimbursement amount would be advanced to the employee (e.g., $100 or $200) as a business expense petty cash fund. As the employee incurs business-related expenses, receipts and/or mileage statements would be kept to be turned in to the treasurer. When they are turned in, the amounts are refunded to the employee's business expense petty cash fund, bringing it back up to the original advance amount. Ultimately, any unused portion of the advance needs to be returned to the church employer.

Taxes

By following these procedures, the actual salary is clearly separated from the business expense reimbursements that do not need to be reported on Form W-2. The employee does not need to worry about deducting these business expenses or substantiating them on his or her annual tax return. Since the amount is not reported as income nor deducted on the tax return, the return is greatly simplified and less likely to be audited. If the return is audited, there will generally be no complicated justification of business expenses, since they were substantiated to the treasurer with receipts and/or mileage statements according to IRS regulations when they were reimbursed.

The Church-Owned Automobile

Some churches provide some or all of their staff with the use of a church-owned vehicle. When an employee uses a church-owned vehicle for both business and personal use, certain procedures are required for tax purposes. (Personal use generally includes commuting between home and the church.)

The employee must keep adequate records of the business-use miles for which the church-owned car is driven. The records for business miles should indicate date, purpose, destination, and miles for all business transportation/travel. It is not enough to just keep personal-use miles. The total miles the car is driven during the year should be determined based on odometer readings at the beginning and end of the year. Total miles driven less business miles provides the personal miles on which to determine personal-use value.

If the employee fully reimburses the employer for the "value" of the personal use of the vehicle, then no "value" would be reported as taxable income on Form W-2. *Otherwise, the "value" of personal use of a church-owned vehicle is a taxable benefit to the employee* and must be included on an employee's Form W-2. Income tax is not required to be withheld for lay employees as long as the employer advises all employees that no withholding will be done for the "value" of the benefit. Notification must be made by January 1 of the year in which no withholding will be done. FICA social security taxes *must be* withheld on the full amount of the "value added" for each staff member affected who is not ordained or district licensed.

The "value" of the availability of a church-owned vehicle to be added to Form W-2 (or reimbursed to the employer by the employee) is the *cost to the employee* of renting or leasing a comparable *vehicle.* The IRS has standard tables that determine the annual lease value of a vehicle based on the vehicle's fair market value. The "value" of the fuel used is another benefit that must be added if the church pays for all the fuel. An employer should contact the IRS (1-800-TAX-FORM) and request the most recent information when determining these values for tax and income reporting purposes (IRS Publication 535, *Business Expenses*).

Likewise, the church governing board and staff of any church providing vehicles to employees for both personal and business use will want to work closely with their personal tax advisers to make certain the "value" of the benefit is determined and reported properly.

Documentation of Mileage

Regardless of the method in which auto expenses are handled, accurate and detailed written records are essential to document the following: the amount of expense and/or mileage, the time and place of transportation/travel, and the business purpose. The taxpayer is required to have "adequate records" or "sufficient evidence" to support the taxpayer's own statement. The best method is to keep a detailed daily log.

Depreciation Restrictions

Rules governing depreciation deductions for automobiles continue to change. Certain transition rules may be applicable to some situations. If you are using depreciation under the actual-expense auto deduction rules, work closely with your personal tax advisers.

Taxes

Summary

In minimizing taxes for all church employees, proper handling of tax-free employee benefits and reimbursements for business transportation/travel and other business and professional expenses are vital. However, these require careful planning and proper action of the local church board or governing committee. Specific guidelines and accounting standards are available from the IRS (1-800-TAX-FORM).

Those *employee benefits* that can be considered tax-free should be paid directly by the church and not reimbursed.

4
BUDGETING, REPORTING, AND FINANCIAL AUDITS

▶ (Note: The CD accompanying this book has an electronic version of a church budget [ChurchBudget] pictured on the next page. Buyers of *The Church Treasurer's Manual* are free to alter the sample per the needs of their local churches and use it as a daily operating budget. This chapter will refer to the sample budget for purposes of illustration.)

Just as an individual doesn't *have* to keep a home budget to run the finances of his or her personal life, a church doesn't *have* to have a budget unless it wants to exist for more than a short time.

A church's budget gives the organization a set direction and allows for periodic maintenance and adjustment when *expected* income and *actual* income differ. The budget allows a church to set its goals into concrete terms and divide the financial resources into appropriate categories.

Different-sized churches use budgets differently, so it will be important for the treasurer to make sure the budget he or she prepares works well. For instance, larger churches might have budget categories for rental properties and investment income. But the chances of smaller churches having many of these kinds of accounts are slim. The budget of a smaller church does not need to be overly complicated to account for potential categories that are not likely to be part of its reality.

HOW DO YOU DETERMINE THE ANNUAL BUDGET?

A church's annual budget is typically set in accordance with previous year's expenses and consultation with each department.

THE CHURCH TREASURER'S MANUAL

BUDGET INPUT LEDGER

	A	B	C	D	E
1	G/A General Ledger				
2					
3	Acct.				
4	No.	Account Name	Balance Forward	Current Activity	Balance
5	-----	-------------------------------	-----------------	-----------------	-----------------
6	1010	CASH IN BANK	($107.60)	($1,249.19)	($1,356.79)
7	1060	CASH ADVANCE - YOUTH PASTOR	$100.00	$0.00	$100.00
8	1070	CASH ADVANCE - VBS	$50.00	$0.00	$50.00
9	2030	FICA TAX	($13.78)	$0.21	($13.57)
10	2040	FEDERAL INCOME TAX	$30.00	$0.00	$30.00
11	2050	STATE INCOME TAX	$0.00	$0.00	$0.00
12	3010	GENERAL OPERATING FUND	$0.00	$0.00	$0.00
13	3011	CURRENT YEAR OPERATING FUND	($133.94)	$1,470.11	$1,336.17
14	3012	PRIOR YEAR'S DEFICIT (SURPLUS)	$0.00	$0.00	$0.00
15	3020	MISSION FUND	$0.00	$0.00	$0.00
16	3011	CURRENT YEAR MISSION FUND	$0.00	$0.00	$0.00
17	3012	PRIOR YEAR'S DEFICIT (SURPLUS)	$0.00	$0.00	$0.00
18	3030	EXPANSION FUND	$0.00	$0.00	$0.00
19	3011	CURRENT YEAR EXPANSION FUND	$0.00	$0.00	$0.00
20	3012	PRIOR YEAR'S DEFICIT (SURPLUS)	$0.00	$0.00	$0.00
21	3040	YOUTH PASTOR'S YOUTH FUND	$0.00	$0.00	$0.00
22	3050	WOMEN'S MINISTRIES	$0.00	$0.00	$0.00
23	3060	MEN'S MINISTRIES	$0.00	$0.00	$0.00
24	3070	ORGAN FUND	$0.00	$0.00	$0.00
25	3080	MORTGAGE RETIREMENT	$0.00	$0.00	$0.00
26	3090	NOT USED	$0.00	$0.00	$0.00
27	3097	GYM RESERVE	$0.00	$0.00	$0.00
28	3098	BUS PAINTING	$0.00	$0.00	$0.00
29	3100	NOT USED	$0.00	$0.00	$0.00
30	3110	NOT USED	$0.00	$0.00	$0.00
31	3120	TEENS	$0.00	$0.00	$0.00
32	3130	NOT USED	$0.00	$0.00	$0.00
33	3140	NOT USED	$0.00	$0.00	$0.00
34		INCOME ACCOUNTS			$0.00
35	4011	TITHES AND OFFERINGS	($45,979.23)	($9,504.40)	($55,483.63)
36	4022	EXPANSION FUND	($1,666.00)	($247.50)	($1,913.50)
37	4033	MISSION FUND	($3,961.51)	($775.00)	($4,736.51)
38	4043	OTHER MISSIONS	($173.98)	$0.00	($173.98)
39	4044	OTHER MISSIONS	$0.00	$0.00	$0.00
40	4052	RENTAL RECEIPTS	($11,000.00)	($1,500.00)	($12,500.00)
41	4053	GYMNASIUM RENTAL INCOME	$0.00	$0.00	$0.00
42		EXPENSE ACCOUNTS			$0.00
43	5011	DENOMINATIONAL BUDGET	$0.00	$0.00	$0.00
44	5012	NOT USED	$0.00	$0.00	$0.00
45	5021	P AND B (PENSIONS AND BENEFITS)	$0.00	$0.00	$0.00
46	5031	LOCAL DISTRICT EXPENSES	$0.00	$0.00	$0.00
47	5041	COLLEGE SUPPORT	$0.00	$0.00	$0.00
48	6011	FIRE AND LIABILITY INSURANCE	$2,208.52	$466.50	$2,675.02
49	6021	NOT USED	$0.00	$0.00	$0.00
50	6031	CHURCH VAN INSURANCE	$240.50	$0.00	$240.50
51	6041	NOT USED	$0.00	$0.00	$0.00
52	6051	UMBRELLA INSURANCE	$0.00	$0.00	$0.00
53	6061	HOMEOWNERS INSURANCE	$0.00	$0.00	$0.00
54	6101	ELECTRIC	$5,126.50	$1,706.79	$6,833.29
55	6111	TELEPHONE	$936.47	$174.13	$1,110.60
56	6121	WATER	$1,140.78	$358.28	$1,499.06
57	6131	GAS	$80.16	$40.58	$120.74
58	6141	TRASH	$489.75	$97.95	$587.70
59	6151	PARSONAGE ELECTRIC	$261.59	$0.00	$261.59
60	6161	PARSONAGE TELEPHONE	$0.00	$0.00	$0.00
61	6171	PARSONAGE WATER	$115.50	$0.00	$115.50
62	6181	PARSONAGE GAS	$83.	$0.00	.19
63	6201	GENERAL MAINTENA	$2,33	$701.59	
64	6211	RENOVATION EXP		$0.00	
65	?31	CAPITAL EXPEN			
6?		PARSONAGE M			
		'URCH VAN			

Fig. 4.1

Budgeting, Reporting, and Financial Audits

Most churches have a board or oversight committee that approves the budget, sometimes in conjunction with a subcommittee responsible for the church's finances.

If the treasurer or the church decides that each department needs its own budget accounts, the treasurer should consult with the head of each department and request a formal budget proposal for the coming year. The budget proposal should list every expense the department anticipates in the coming year, with smaller, catchall categories for items such as supplies.

❢ It is often helpful for those in charge of each department to receive a copy of the previous year's budget and actual expenses to help them make estimates for the new budget. While it is advisable to review the previous year's budget, do not budget solely on past experience but also on future goals and objectives.

Once the treasurer receives all budget proposals from the various departments, that person combines them all into a master budget and usually submits it to the church's governing board or financial oversight committee. After negotiations between each department head and the financial oversight committee, a final budget is established.

What's a finance committee? A finance committee is a committee usually established by the local church's governing board. This committee combines one or more members from the governing board with other congregants. The finance committee, as its name implies, is responsible for the financial direction and security of the church. The church treasurer reports to the finance committee.

> What's a finance committee? A finance committee is a committee usually established by the local church's governing board. This committee combines one or more members from the governing board with other congregants. The finance committee, as its name implies, is responsible for the financial direction and security of the church. The church treasurer reports to the finance committee.

(Note: while it is most common for the various departments in churches to not have to raise all their own funds, in some churches the Sunday School, youth, or mission departments are required to raise a portion of their own funds through offerings or fund-raising. In these cases the church budget should have separate income and expense accounts for each department.)

THE CHART OF ANNUAL ACCOUNTS

When the treasurer is setting up a list of accounts, there are a number of things to keep in mind. First, most denominations require reporting from the local church regarding certain accounts (mission budgets, budgets that support the denomination, budgets that support local districts, etc.). Before setting up a list of accounts, a treasurer should check with his or her denomination to determine what specifications exist for reporting purposes, then include specific line items to account for those requirements.

In the sample budget (fig. 4.1), a church is required to report its overall denominational expenses (account 5011), the pastor's pension expenses (account 5021), expenses for its local district (account 5031), and denominational college support expenses (account 5041). The treasurer could have simply put all these expenses into a single account called "Denominational Expenses." If he or she had done that, when the time came for the year-end reports to the denomination, the treasurer would have a lot of work in going back over all the charges to that account and separating them into the categories required for the reports. It is much easier to track the expenses by the required categories throughout the year than it is to do it after the fact at the end of the year.

One area treasurers sometimes neglect when setting up a list of accounts is taxes. Sometimes churches have a laissez-faire attitude toward taxes, sensing that since they are nonprofit organizations, taxes will not substantially apply to them. However, the IRS makes no distinction between for-profit companies and nonprofit organizations regarding the payment of FICA taxes. Anytime

Budgeting, Reporting, and Financial Audits

taxes are not disbursed as required by the IRS, the treasurer could become *personally* liable.

❢ **When the treasurer is setting up the list of accounts, it is a good idea to leave a lot of room between ledger numbers identifying each account. For instance, if the budget account for the church vehicle expenses is numbered 1500, it is a good idea to follow it with an account numbered 1510 or even 1550. Then when an atypical major expense (such as painting the church bus) occurs and it is really too large to put in the "miscellaneous" account, there is room to add it after the vehicle account and before the next major category.**

Most churches will have many different types of accounts depending on the expenses associated with churches of their size. However, every church will have a budget category titled "Income." (All funds coming into the church fall into this area. Often churches will set up several line items under the "Income" category to include different types of income such as tithes, funds for building campaigns, mission funds, etc.) Other standard budget accounts include the following:

- Property and Equipment (utilities, insurance on property, maintenance)
- Debt
- Personnel (anyone to whom funds are disbursed, including lawn and maintenance service, gifts to staff, nursery attendants, insurance, etc.)
- General Expenses (including special events, entertainment, retreats and conferences, pastor's car)
- Operating Expenses (office supplies, postage, printing)

Other types of accounts treasurers sometimes use include missions expenses, outreach expenses, and church expansion expenses. These are included on the sample budget to give you an idea of what some full budgets look like.

It is advisable to keep a tight reign on the size of your overall line items in your income accounts. Churches often receive and sometimes request special offerings. These funds may be given for anything from sponsoring a youth trip to helping provide new supplies for the church kitchen. The possibilities are endless. If the treasurer lets these types of funds accrue over long periods of time, there are several potential problems. Sometimes the special funds received get mixed in with all other general offerings, and the treasurer loses track of how much was given for special purposes. Treasurers who attempt to track all special funds with separate line items in the Income account may find after several months that the list of items is very large and each line contains very little income.

💡 When giving is earmarked for special items, disburse those funds for their intended purposes as quickly as possible. This will avoid funds sitting around for years causing headaches for the treasurer who must continually account for them.

FINANCIAL REPORTS TO THE CONGREGATION

The annual budget for the congregation has been approved, and the various accounts of the accounting system (chart of accounts) has been established. The basis around which the financial data of the congregation is prepared is in place. The treasurer must now transform this data into meaningful reports so that the financial progress of the congregation can be monitored and decisions made.

- At the very minimum the financial statements should consist of a balance sheet and statement of revenue and expense (also called a statement of activity).
- The financial statements should be designed to meet the needs of the user.
- Financial reports should be prepared on a timely basis.
- The format should be simple and easily understood.

Budgeting, Reporting, and Financial Audits

- The reports should be all-inclusive.
- The reports should have a point of comparison—comparison to budget or comparison to last year.
- Reports should provide the needed detail for decision making.
- The treasurer should accompany the financial reports with a verbal or written report that points out critical items and areas. (See Appendix 2 for sample reports.)

A list of different types of reports includes these:

Balance Sheet

The balance sheet is the financial report that shows the financial position of an organization at a given point in time. It summarizes the assets, liabilities, and fund balance.

Statement of Revenue and Expense

The income and expense report is the financial report that provides a summary of the operating results of a fund during a specific period of time. Income and expense reports may be shown in great detail or may be shown in a summarized manner depending on the needs of the user.

Statement of Cash Flows

The statement of cash flows provides a summary of the sources and uses of funds during a specific period of time. In other words, it provides an outline about the cash receipts and cash disbursements.

Other Financial Reports

In addition to the above statements, there are many other reports that congregations find useful. Each individual congregation should assess its situation periodically and determine the extent and scope of its reporting needs. A report preparer should always keep in mind the needs of the user. Financial reports that do not communicate and do not get used are not doing the job. If an audience needs simple reports, the preparer should keep them simple but highlight the critical information. If an audience requires more detail, make sure the reports provide it in a format that doesn't overwhelm them (Evangelical Lutheran 2007, chapter 14).

AUDITS*

Church board members have a *long* list of responsibilities. Among these is the responsibility for the money that flows through the church. It's such an important issue that an annual audit of the church's records is a must. Sometimes treasurers may see audits as somewhat insulting, as if the church doesn't trust its treasurer. However, an audit is really a confirmation of what a good job the treasurer is doing and actually protects the treasurer against any charges of financial mishandling. External audits are performed by an independent auditor who has no impairing relationship to the church and thus can review its data procedures with maximum objectivity. Internal audits generally are performed by church members or by persons closely associated with the church.

Why Have an Audit?
- To abide by the general rules of many denominations that *mandate* that their churches have audits
- "To obtain independent assurance that all financial records fairly represent the financial condition of the church"
- "To [ensure] that the year's financial activity has been properly recorded in accordance with generally accepted accounting principles [GAAP]"
- "To [ensure] adherence with the policies and procedures established by the congregation"
- "To maintain confidence in the integrity of the congregation's

---

*Quotation-marked material in this section is from Evangelical Lutheran 2007, chapter 15.

financial system and the persons responsible for handling the finances"
- To set habits of fiscal responsibility to assure that when there is turnover in personnel, there will be continuity in accountability and nothing will fall through the cracks

External Audits

The ideal audit method is to have an annual audit performed by independent CPAs. However, only large churches generally can afford this extra expense. External audits of smaller churches often are done on a non-Generally Accepted Accounting Principles (GAAP) basis—the statements do not conform to the full accrual method with depreciation recognized. Non-GAAP financial statements for smaller churches often are acceptable to banks and other agencies.

Internal Audits

Members of the church may form an audit committee to perform an internal audit to determine the validity of the financial statements. (Sample internal audit guidelines for churches follow below.) If the committee takes its task seriously, the result may be significant improvements in internal control and accounting procedures. Too often, the internal audit committee only conducts a cursory review, commends the treasurer for a job well done, and provides the church with a false sense of security.

The internal audit committee is appointed by the church's governing board. This committee should be composed of at least two members of the congregation, excluding the treasurer and the financial secretary. The board preferably should select individuals who have had training in accounting procedures but do not handle any of the church's funds.

The Audit Committee

- "examines and reviews all accounts and records;

- "exercises supervision and oversees the work of this review if it is conducted by an outside accounting firm;
- "examines all insurance policies and prepares a schedule of the insurance coverage;
- "inspects and examines securities and investments;
- "prepares a schedule of the securities and investments for review by the finance committee;
- "reports its findings in writing to the church council with supporting schedules and recommendations for change and improvement;
- "verifies that the congregation complies with federal and state tax laws and regulations."

Audit Procedures

1. *"Review the Recording of Cash Receipts"*
    - Are the cash handling procedures in writing?
    - "Trace deposits from the counter's reports in the financial secretary's and treasurer's records. Compare these to the entries recording such deposits so they agree with the deposits recorded by the bank."
    - "Check on the timeliness of the deposits."
    - "On a sample basis, check the account distribution in the cash receipts journal, being especially alert for funds designated for specific purposes."
    - Are Sunday School offerings properly recorded and delivered to the money counters?
    - Are procedures established to care for offerings and monies delivered or mailed to the church office between Sundays?
    - Are at least two members of the counting committee present when offerings are counted? (The persons counting the money should not include the pastor or the church treasurer.)
    - Is it standard procedure for money counters to verify that the contents of the offering envelopes are identical to the amounts written on the outside of the envelopes?

Budgeting, Reporting, and Financial Audits

- Are all checks stamped with a restrictive endorsement stamp immediately after the offering envelope contents are verified?
- Are money counters rotated so the same people are not handling the funds each week?
- Are donor-restricted funds properly identified during the process of counting offerings?
- Are restricted funds held for the intended purpose(s) and not spent on operating needs?
- Are two members of the offering counting team in custody of the offering until it is deposited in the bank, placed in a night depository, or locked in the church's safe?
- Are all funds promptly deposited? Compare offering and other receipt records with bank deposits.
- Are all receipts deposited intact? Receipts should not be used to pay cash expenses.

2. *"Verify Check Accounting"*
   - "Inspect the cash expenditures record in the cash disbursement journal that should show the date, check number, name of payee, amount of check, and account distribution for each check written."
   - "Check mathematical accuracy of entries."
   - "Examine the authority for writing a check such as approval on invoices; pastor's call, including current salary and housing arrangements; employee salaries and contract agreements; actions of council reported in minutes; and actual receipts for tangible goods."
   - "Examine canceled checks to verify that disbursements were actually paid to the proper parties."
   - Are all disbursements paid by check except for minor expenditures paid through the petty cash fund?
   - Is written documentation available to support all disbursements?

- If a petty cash fund is used, are vouchers prepared for each disbursement from the fund?
- Are prenumbered checks used? Account for all the check numbers, including voided checks.
- Are blank checks ever signed in advance? (This should never be done.)
- "Prepare a statement of expenditures for comparison with the adopted budget for the year, and analyze variances."
- "Analyze expenditures, noting proper capitalization of major improvements, refurbishing, new equipment, and proper designation of employees vs. independent contractors."

3. *"Reconcile Bank Accounts"*
   - "Inspect, on a sample basis, endorsements on the canceled checks."
   - Request banks, savings and loan associations, and other investment agents to confirm, in writing, the balances held in accounts.
   - Make sure those signing checks are the same as those with signature cards on file with your financial institutions.
   - Obtain the bank statement for the first month after year-end directly from the bank for review by the audit committee. Otherwise, obtain the last bank statement from the church treasurer.
   - "Prepare a statement of reconciliation between bank balances and balances shown on the books. The reconciliation should begin with the bank's balance. Add to that figure deposits shown on the books but not yet credited on the bank statement. Subtract the outstanding checks (those that have not yet cleared the bank) to prove the balance shown on the books."
   - Are written bank reconciliations prepared on a timely basis? Test the reconciliation for the last month in the fiscal year. Trace transactions between the bank and the books for completeness and timeliness.

Budgeting, Reporting, and Financial Audits

- Are there any checks that have been outstanding over three months?
- Are there any unusual transactions in the bank statement immediately following year-end?
- The statement of reconciliation should be performed by someone who does not process receipts or disbursements.

4. *"Examine Petty Cash Funds"*
   - Is a petty cash fund used for disbursements of a small amount?
   - Do the disbursement vouchers have proper approval and receipts?
   - Are the reimbursements to the fund made properly?
   - Have maximum figures for individual payments been established and followed?

5. *"Examine Individual Member Records"*
   - Are individual donor records kept as a basis to provide donor acknowledgments for all single contributions of $250 or more?
   - If no goods or services were provided (other than intangible religious benefits) in exchange for a gift, does the receipt include a statement to this effect?
   - If goods or services (other than intangible religious benefits) were provided in exchange for a gift, does the receipt
     - ▶ inform the donor that the amount of the contribution deductible for federal income tax purposes is limited to the excess of the amount of any money and the value of any property contributed by the donor over the value of the goods and services provided by the organization and
     - ▶ provide the donor with a good-faith estimate of the value of such goods and services?
   - Although not required by the IRS, has your church adopted a policy of issuing an annual contribution report to donors listing at least each week's donations? If not, each donation?

- Are the donations traced from the weekly counting sheets to the donor records for a selected time period by the audit committee?

6. *"Inspect Insurance Policies, and Prepare a Schedule of Insurance in Effect to Show the Following"*
   - "Effective and expiration dates"
   - "Kind and classification of coverage"
   - "Maximum amounts of each coverage"
   - "Premium amounts and terms"
   - "Comparison of insurance coverage with the insurance appraisal or other supporting cost data. Does insurance coverage provide adequate replacement value for the church building and personal equipment, such as the organ, pews, hymnals, computers, printers, [and so on]?"
   - Is workers' compensation insurance being carried as provided by law in most states? Are all employees (and perhaps some independent contractors) covered under the workers' compensation policy?

7. *Inspect Savings and Investment Accounts*
   - Are all savings and investment accounts recorded in the financial records? Compare monthly statements to the books.
   - Are earnings or losses from savings and investment accounts recorded in the books?

8. *Examine Land, Buildings, and Equipment Records*
   - Are there detailed records of land, buildings, and equipment, including date acquired, description, and cost or fair market value at date of acquisition?
   - Was an equipment physical inventory taken at year-end?
   - Have the property records been reconciled to the insurance coverages?

Budgeting, Reporting, and Financial Audits

9. *Inspect Accounts Payable*
   - Is there a schedule of unpaid invoices, including vendor name, invoice date, and due date?
   - Are any of the accounts payable items significantly past due?
   - Are there any disputes with vendors over amounts owed?

10. *Inspect Personnel Records*
    - Does the church maintain the following documents?
        - ▶ Applications for employment
        - ▶ W-4s and other tax forms
        - ▶ Personnel files
        - ▶ Performance appraisal and evaluation forms
        - ▶ Employee handbook
        - ▶ Immigration I-9 forms

11. *Ascertain Compliance with Federal Reporting Obligations*
    - Does the church file on a timely basis the following forms if applicable?
        - ▶ Federal payroll tax forms (Form 941, Form W-2, Form W-3, Form 1099-MISC)
        - ▶ Donee information returns (Form 8282)
        - ▶ Annual certification of racial nondiscrimination for Christian schools (Form 5578) (Pensions n.d., Memo 8)

    Upon completion of the audit report, it is suggested that a certification be completed and made a part of the congregation's records indicating that a review of the financial records has been performed.

WORKS CITED

Busby, Dan. 2007. *The Zondervan Church and Nonprofit Tax & Financial Guide: 2008 Edition.* Grand Rapids: Zondervan.

Church of God (Anderson, Ind.). 2002. *Church Treasurer* (www.benefitsboard.com). 1 March.

Divisions of Finance/Operations. 1996. *Finance Manual for Alliance Church Treasurers.* Colorado Springs: Christian Missionary Alliance.

Evangelical Lutheran Church of America. 2002. *Resources for Congregational Treasurers and Bookkeepers* (www.elca.org/treasurer/congregations/responsibilities.html).

Kavanaugh, Lee Hill. 2002. "Theft Tests Small Church." *Kansas City Star,* 7 April, A1.

Pensions and Benefits USA. n.d. *Tax Helps Memos 1-12.* Kansas City: Pensions and Benefits USA.

APPENDIX 1

WHERE TO GO FOR MORE INFORMATION

Denominations

American Baptists: www.abcusamissions.org/missiongiving/treasurer.cfm

Church of God, Cleveland: www.benefitsboard.com

Church of the Nazarene: www.nazarene.org/pensions/index.html

Evangelical Covenant Church: www.covchurch.org/cov/financial/12C.html

Evangelical Lutheran Church in America: www.elca.org/treasurer

Church of the United Brethren in Christ: www.ub.org/forchurches/PRC Manual/index.html

United Church of Christ: www.ucc.org/finance/index.html

United Methodist: www.umc.org/churchleadership/layministry/resource/treasurer.htm

General Information

Church Bytes Software Guide, Church Bytes, Inc., 562 Brightleaf Square No. 9, 905 West Main Street, Durham, NC 27702; phone: 919-479-5242

Christian Ministry Finance Onliners: clubs.yahoo.com/clubs/financemgtat ministries (requires free registration)

Church Finance Today (a monthly review of accounting, financial, and tax developments affecting ministers and clergy), published by *Christianity Today:* www.churchfinancetoday.com

Church Law & Tax Report (a bimonthly review of legal and tax developments affecting ministers and churches), published by *Christianity Today:* www.churchfinancetoday.com

Church and Clergy Tax Guide (book, updated annually), published by *Christianity Today:* www.churchfinancetoday.com

Financial Management software catalog:
www.npinfotech.org/tnopsi/finance/fnindex.htm

Nazarene Treasury System: osprey@flash.net

Treasurer's Discussion Board: cmr.gospelcom.net/cgi-cmr/bbs/bbs_forum.cgi?forum=ad_fina

www.bcidot.org

Zondervan Church and Nonprofit Tax & Financial Guide and *Zondervan Minister's Tax & Financial Guide,* published annually. Available at your local Christian bookstore or www.ECFA.org

APPENDIX 2

FINANCIAL FORMS

Offering Report Form

Date _____

CASH	A.M. Amount	P.M. Amount
$		
$ 20.00		
$ 10.00		
$ 5.00		
$ 1.00		
TOTAL		

COINS	A.M. Amount	P.M. Amount
$ 0.50		
$ 0.25		
$ 0.10		
$ 0.05		
$ 0.01		
TOTAL		

CHECKS

NAME	AMOUNT
A.M. TOTAL	

NAME	AMOUNT
P.M. TOTAL	

SUMMARY

TOTALS:	A.M.	P.M.	TOTALS
Cash			
Coin			
Checks			
TOTALS:			

Counted by:

Breakdown of Receipts

	TITHES	SUNDAY SCHOOL	MISSIONS				TOTALS
A.M.							
P.M.							
TOTALS							

THE CHURCH TREASURER'S MANUAL

Individual Contributions Record

Name _____   Envelope Number _____

20__	Tithes	Other Giving		Total
Week		Item	Amount	
1				
2				
3				
4				
5				
6				
7				
8				
9				
10				
11				
12				
13				
1st Quarter				
Year-to-date				
14				
15				
16				
17				
18				
19				
20				
21				
22				
23				
24				
25				
26				
2nd Quarter				
Year-to-date				

20__	Tithes	Other Giving	Total
Week			
27			
28			
29			
30			
31			
32			
33			
34			
35			
36			
37			
38			
39			
3rd Quarter			
Year-to-date			
40			
41			
42			
43			
44			
45			
46			
47			
48			
49			
50			
51			
52			
4th Quarter			
Year-to-date			

The only goods and services provided in exchange for these contributions are intangible religious benefits.

_____   _____
Church Treasurer   Date

Appendix 2

Check Request Form

Church Name
Treasurer name, Treasurer
Church address
City, State, Zip

Pay to: _____

AMOUNT: _____ Check # _____

Date	Description	Account	Amount

Submitted by: _____

Approved by: _____
Note: Church Board approval must be obtained prior to expenditure.

Church Name
Treasurer Name, Treasurer
Address
City, State, Zip

Pay to: _____

AMOUNT: _____ Check # _____

Date	Description	Account	Amount

Submitted by: _____

Approved by: _____
Note: Church Board approval must be obtained prior to expenditure.

Sample Charitable Gift Receipt*

Receipt No. 1

Received from: Howard K. Auburn

Cash received as an absolute gift:

Date Cash Received	Amount Received
1/2/08	$250.00
1/16/08	50.00
3/13/08	300.00
3/27/08	100.00
6/12/08	500.00
7/10/08	150.00
8/21/08	200.00
10/16/08	400.00
11/20/08	350.00
	$2,300.00

Any goods or services you may have received in connection with this gift were solely intangible religious benefits.

> *(Note: It is very important for a religious organization to use wording of this nature when no goods or services were given in exchange for the gift.)*

This document is necessary for any available federal income tax deduction for your contribution. Please retain it for your records.

Receipt issued on: January 10, 2009

Receipt issued by: Harold Morrison, Treasurer
Castleview Church
1008 High Drive
Dover, DE 19901

1. This sample receipt is based on the following assumptions:
    a. Goods or services were provided in exchange for the gifts.
    b. The receipt is issued on a periodic or annual basis for all gifts whether over or under $250.
2. All receipts should be numbered consecutively for control and accounting purposes.

---

*Reprinted by permission from *The Zondervan Church and Nonprofit Tax & Financial Guide: 2008 Edition* by Dan Busby, CPA (Grand Rapids: Zondervan, 2007), 163.

Appendix 2

Sample Charitable Gift Receipt*

Receipt No. 2

Received from: Charles K. Vandell
Cash received:

Date Cash Received	Gross Amount Received	Value of Goods or Services	Net Charitable Contribution
1/23/08	$80.00	$25.00[1]	$ 55.00
3/20/08	300.00		300.00
4/24/08	60.00		60.00
6/19/08	500.00	100.00[2]	400.00
9/04/08	275.00		275.00
10/30/08	200.00		200.00
12/18/08	1,000.00		1,000.00
			$2,290.00

Property received described as follows:
Received on October 22, 2008, 12 brown Samsonite folding chairs.

In return for certain gifts listed above, we provided you with the following goods or services (our estimate of the fair market value is indicated):
 (1) Christian music tapes $25.00
 (2) Limited edition art print $100.00

You may have also received intangible religious benefits, but these benefits do not need to be valued for tax purposes.

The deductible portion of your contribution for federal income tax purposes is limited to the excess of your contribution over the value of goods and services we provided to you.

This document is necessary for any available federal income tax deduction for your contribution. Please retain it for your records.

Receipt issued on: January 15, 2009

Receipt issued by: Harold Morrison, Treasurer
                     Castleview Church
                     1008 High Drive
                     Dover, DE 19901

1. This sample receipt is based on the following assumptions:
   a. Goods or services were provided in exchange for the gifts.
   b. The receipt is issued on a periodic or annual basis for all gifts whether over or under $250.
2. All receipts should be numbered consecutively for control and accounting purposes.

---

*Reprinted by permission from *The Zondervan Church and Nonprofit Tax & Financial Guide: 2008 Edition* by Dan Busby, CPA (Grand Rapids: Zondervan, 2007), 179.

Sample Letter to Noncash Donors*

Noncash Acknowledgment No. 1

Charitable Gift Receipt for Noncash Gifts
(other than for autos, boats, or airplanes)

RETAIN FOR INCOME TAX PURPOSES

(All acknowledgments should be numbered consecutively for control and accounting purposes.)

Donor's name and address

Date Acknowledgment Issued

Thank you for your noncash gift as follows:
    Date of gift:
    Description of gift:
    (Note: No value is shown for the gift. Valuation is the responsibility of the donor.)

    To substantiate your gift for IRS purposes, the tax law requires that this acknowledgment state whether you have received any goods or services in exchange for the gift. You have received no goods or services. *(Note: If goods or services were provided to the donor, replace the previous sentence with:* In return for your contribution, you have received the following goods or services: _(description)_ , which we value at (good-faith estimate) . The value of the goods and services you received must be deducted from the value of your contribution to determine your charitable deduction.)

    If your noncash gifts for the year total more than $500, you must include Form 8283 (a copy of Form 8283 and its instructions are enclosed for your convenience) with your income tax return. Section A is used to report gifts valued at $5,000 or under. You can complete Section A on your own. When the value of the gift is more than $5,000, you will need to have the property appraised. The appraiser's findings are reported in Section B of Form 8283. The rules also apply if you give "similar items of property" with a total value above $5,000—even if you gave the items to different charities. Section B of Form 8283 must be signed by the appraiser. It is essential to attach the form to your tax return.

    You might want an appraisal (even if your gift does not require one) in case you have to convince the IRS of the property's worth. You never need an appraisal or an appraisal summary for gifts of publicly traded securities, even if their total value exceeds $5,000. You must report those gifts (when the value is more than $500) by completing Section A of Form 8283 and attaching it to your return.

    For gifts of publicly traded stock, an appraisal is not required. For gifts of closely held stock, an appraisal is not required if the value of the stock is under $10,000, but part of the appraisal summary form must be completed if the value is over $5,000. If the gift is valued over $10,000, then both an appraisal and an appraisal summary form are required.

    If we receive a gift of property subject to the appraisal summary rules, we must report to both the IRS and you if we dispose of the gift within three years. We do not have to notify the IRS or you if we dispose of a gift that did not require an appraisal summary.

    Again, we are grateful for your generous contribution. Please let us know if we can give you and your advisors more information about the IRS's reporting requirements.

Your Nonprofit Organization

---

*Reprinted by permission from *The Zondervan Church and Nonprofit Tax & Financial Guide: 2008 Edition* by Dan Busby, CPA (Grand Rapids: Zondervan, 2007), 164.

Appendix 2

Travel and Other Expense Reimbursement Policy*

Purpose

The Board of [name of church] recognizes that pastors and other staff ("Personnel") of [name of church] may be required to travel or incur other expenses from time to time to conduct ministry business and to further the mission of this church. The purpose of this Policy is to ensure that (a) adequate cost controls are in place, and that (b) travel and other expenditures are appropriate, and (c) to provide a uniform and consistent approach for the timely reimbursement of authorized expenses incurred by Personnel. It is the policy of [name of church] to reimburse only reasonable and necessary expenses actually incurred by Personnel.

When incurring business expenses, [name of church] expects Personnel to

- Exercise discretion and good business judgment with respect to those expenses
- Be cost conscious and spend ministry money as carefully and judiciously as the individual would spend his or her own funds
- Report expenses, supported by required documentation, as they were actually spent

Expense Report

Expenses will not be reimbursed unless the individual requesting reimbursement submits a written Expense Report. The Expense Report, which shall be submitted at least monthly or within two weeks of the completion of travel if travel expense reimbursement is requested, must include

- The individual's name
- The date, origin, destination, and purpose of the trip, including a description of each organization-related activity during the trip
- The name and affiliation of all people for whom expenses are claimed (i.e., people on whom money is spent in order to conduct [name of church]'s business)
- An itemized list of all expenses for which reimbursement is requested

---

*Reprinted, with minor adaptation, by permission from *The Zondervan Church and Nonprofit Tax & Financial Guide: 2008 Edition* by Dan Busby, CPA (Grand Rapids: Zondervan, 2007), 78-81.

Receipts

Receipts are required for all expenditures billed directly to [name of church], such as airfare and hotel charges. No expense in excess of $_____ will be reimbursed to Personnel unless the individual requesting reimbursement submits with the Expense Report written receipts from each vendor (not a credit card receipt or statement) showing the vendor's name, a description of the services provided (if not otherwise obvious), the date, and the total expenses, including tips (if applicable).

General Travel Requirements

- **Necessity of travel.** In determining the reasonableness and necessity of travel expenses, Personnel and the person authorizing the travel shall consider the ways in which [name of church] will benefit from the travel and weigh those benefits against the anticipated costs of the travel. The same factors shall be taken into account in deciding whether the benefits to [name of church] outweigh the costs; less expensive alternatives, such as participation by telephone or video conferencing; or the availability of local programs or training opportunities.
- **Personal and spousal travel expenses.** Individuals traveling on behalf of [name of church] may incorporate personal travel or business with their Company-related trips; however, Personnel shall not arrange Church travel at a time that is less advantageous to [name of church] or involving greater expenses to [name of church] in order to accommodate personal travel plans. Any additional expenses incurred as a result of personal travel, including but not limited to extra hotel nights, additional stopovers, meals, or transportation, are the sole responsibility of the individual and will not be reimbursed by [name of church]. Expenses associated with travel of an individual's spouse, family, or friends will not be reimbursed by [name of church].

Air Travel

Air travel reservations should be made as far in advance as possible in order to take advantage of reduced fares.

Frequent-Flyer Miles and Compensation for Denied Boarding

Personnel traveling on behalf of [name of church] may accept and retain frequent-flyer miles and compensation for denied boarding for

Appendix 2

their personal use. Individuals may not deliberately patronize a single airline to accumulate frequent-flyer miles if less expensive comparable tickets are available through another airline.

Lodging

Personnel traveling on behalf of [name of church] may be reimbursed at the single room rate for the reasonable cost of hotel accommodations. Convenience, the cost of staying in the city in which the hotel is located, and proximity to other venues on the individual's itinerary shall be considered in determining reasonableness. Personnel shall make use of available corporate and discount rates for hotels.

Out-of-Town Meals

Personnel traveling on behalf of [name of church] are reimbursed for the reasonable and actual costs of meals (including tips) subject to a maximum per diem meal allowance of $_____ per day and the terms and conditions established by [name of church] relating to the per diem meal allowance.

Ground Transportation

Employees are expected to use the most economical ground transportation appropriate under the circumstances and should generally use the following, in this order of desirability:

- **Courtesy cars.** Many hotels have courtesy cars, which will take you to and from the airport at no charge. Employees should take advantage of this free service whenever possible. Another alternative may be a shuttle or bus.
- **Airport shuttle or bus.** Airport shuttles or buses generally travel to and from all major hotels for a small fee. At major airports such services are as quick as a taxi and considerably less expensive. Airport shuttle or bus services are generally located near the airport's baggage claim area.
- **Taxis.** When courtesy cars and airport shuttles are not available, a taxi is often the next most economical and convenient form of transportation when the trip is for a limited time and minimal mileage is involved. A taxi may also be the most economical mode of transportation between an individual's home and the airport.
- **Rental cars.** Car rentals are expensive, so other forms of transportation should be considered when practical. Employees will

be allowed to rent a car while out of town provided that advance approval has been given by the individual's supervisor and that the cost is less than alternative methods of transportation.

Personal Cars

Personnel are compensated for use of their personal cars when used for ministry business. When individuals use their personal car for such travel, including travel to and from the airport, mileage will be allowed at the currently approved IRS rate per mile.

In the case of individuals using their personal cars to take a trip that would normally be made by air, mileage will be allowed at the currently approved rate; however, the total mileage reimbursement will not exceed the sum of the lowest available round-trip coach airfare.

Parking/Tolls

Parking and toll expenses, including charges for hotel parking, incurred by Personnel traveling on organization business will be reimbursed. The costs of parking tickets, fines, car washes, valet service, and so on, are the responsibility of the employee and will not be reimbursed.

On-airport parking is permitted for short business trips. For extended trips, Personnel should use off-airport facilities.

Entertainment and Business Meetings

Reasonable expenses incurred for business meetings or other types of business-related entertainment will be reimbursed only if the expenditures are approved in advance by [the treasurer or other designated staff member] of [name of church] and qualify as tax-deductible expenses. Detailed documentation for any such expense must be provided, including

- Date and place of entertainment
- Nature of the expense
- Names, titles, and corporate affiliation of those entertained
- A complete description of the business purpose for the activity, including the specific business matter discussed
- Vendor receipts (not credit card receipts or statements) showing the vendor's name, a description of the services provided, date, and total expenses, including tips (if applicable)

Other Expenses

Reasonable ministry-related telephone and fax charges due to absence of Personnel from the individual's place of business are reim-

Appendix 2

bursable. In addition, reasonable and necessary gratuities that are not covered under meals may be reimbursed.

Nonreimbursable Expenditures

[Name of church] maintains a strict policy that expenses in any category that could be perceived as lavish or excessive will not be reimbursed, as such expenses are inappropriate for reimbursement by a church. Expenses that are not reimbursable include, but are not limited to

- Travel insurance.
- First-class tickets or upgrades.
- When lodging accommodations have been arranged by [name of church] and the individual elects to stay elsewhere, reimbursement is made at the amount no higher than the rate negotiated by [name of church]. Reimbursement shall not be made for transportation between the alternate lodging and the meeting site.
- Limousine travel.
- Movie tickets, liquor or bar costs.
- Membership dues at any country club, private club, athletic club, golf club, tennis club, or similar recreational organization.
- Participation in or attendance at golf, tennis, or sporting events, without the advance approval of the chair of the board or his or her designee.
- Purchase of golf clubs or any other sporting equipment.
- Spa or exercise charges.
- Clothing purchases.
- Business conferences and entertainment that are not approved by [treasurer or other designated staff member] of [name of church].
- Valet service.
- Car washes.
- Toiletry articles.
- Expenses for spouses, friends, or relatives. If a spouse, friend, or relative accompanies staff on a trip, it is the responsibility of the staff to determine any added cost for double occupancy and related expenses and to make the appropriate adjustment in the reimbursement request.
- Overnight retreats without the prior approval of the chair of the board or his or her designee.

Sample Credit Card Policies and Procedures*

Objectives
- To allow church personnel access to efficient and alternative means of payment for approved expenses, especially expenses related to business travel and office supplies
- To improve managerial reporting related to credit card purchases
- To improve efficiency and reduce costs of payables processing

Policies
- Church credit cards will be issued to ministers and staff only upon approval of the Finance Committee.
- Credit cards will be used only for business purposes. Personal purchases of any type are not allowed.
- The following purchases are not allowed:
    - Capital equipment and upgrades over $5,000
    - Construction, renovation/installation
    - Items or services on term contracts
    - Maintenance agreements
    - Personal items or loans
    - Purchases involving trade-in of church property
    - Rentals (other than short-term autos)
    - Any items deemed inconsistent with the values of the ministry
- Cash advances on credit cards are not allowed without written permission from the treasurer.
- Cardholders will be required to sign an agreement indicating their acceptance of these terms. Individuals who do not adhere to these policies and procedures will risk revocation of their credit card privileges and/or disciplinary action.

Procedures
- Credit cards may be requested for prospective cardholders by written request (Credit Card Request Form) to the treasurer.
- Detailed receipts must be retained and attached to the credit

---

*Reprinted by permission from *The Zondervan Church and Nonprofit Tax & Financial Guide: 2008 Edition* by Dan Busby, CPA (Grand Rapids: Zondervan, 2007), 82-83.

Appendix 2

card statements. In the case of meals and entertainment, each receipt must include the date, time, names of all persons involved in the purchase, and a brief description of the business purpose of the purchase, in accordance with Internal Revenue Service regulations.

- Monthly statements, with attached detailed receipts, must be submitted to the Treasurer within 10 days of receipt of the statement to enable timely payment of amounts due.
- All monthly statements submitted for payment must include the initials of the cardholder; the signature of the approving staff member, unless the cardholder is himself or herself the staff member; and the date of approval.
- All monthly statements submitted for payment must have the appropriate account number(s) and the associated amounts clearly written on the statement.

CHURCH CARDHOLDER AGREEMENT*

I,_____, hereby acknowledge receipt of the following credit card:

_____ / _____ - _____ - _____ - _____
(Type of credit card)   (Credit card number)

I understand that improper use of this card may result in disciplinary action, as outlined in the Church handbook, as well as personal liability for any improper purchases. As a cardholder, I agree to comply with the terms and conditions of this agreement, including the attached Church Credit Card Policies and Procedures agreement. I will strive to obtain the best value for the Church when purchasing merchandise and/or services with this card.

I acknowledge receipt of said Agreement and Policies/Procedures and confirm that I have read and understand the terms and conditions. I understand that by using the card, I will be making financial commitments on behalf of the Church and that the Church will be liable to [name of credit card company] for all charges made on this card.

As a holder of this Church card, I agree to accept the responsibility and accountability for the protection and proper use of the card, as reflected above. I will return the card to the business administrator or treasurer upon demand during the period of my employment.

I further agree to return the card upon termination of employment. I understand that the card is not to be used for personal purchases, and if the card is used for personal purchases or for purchases for any other entity, the Church will be entitled to reimbursement from me of such purchases and shall be entitled to pursue legal action, if required, to recover the cost of such purchases, together with costs of collection and reasonable attorneys' fees.

Signature _____ Date _____
                    (Cardholder)

Signature _____ Date _____
                    (Treasurer)

---

*Reprinted, with minor adaptation, by permission from *The Zondervan Church and Nonprofit Tax & Financial Guide: 2008 Edition* by Dan Busby, CPA (Grand Rapids: Zondervan, 2007), 83.

Appendix 2

Sample Accountable Expense Reimbursement Plan*

Whereas, Income tax regulations provide that an arrangement between an employee and employer must meet the requirements of business connection, substantiation, and return of excess payments in order to be considered a reimbursement;

Whereas, Plans that meet the three requirements listed above are considered to be accountable plans, and the reimbursed expenses are generally excludable from an employee's gross compensation;

Whereas, Plans that do not meet all the requirements listed above are considered nonaccountable plans, and payments made under such plans are includable in gross employee compensation; and

Whereas, (name of church) desires to establish an accountable expense reimbursement policy in compliance with the income tax regulations;

Resolved, That (name of church) establish an expense reimbursement policy effective _____, 200__, whereby employees serving the church may receive advances for or reimbursement of expenses if

   A. There is a stated business purpose of the expense related to the ministry of the church and the expenses would qualify for deductions for federal income tax purposes if the expenses were not reimbursed

   B. The employee provides adequate substantiation to the church for all expenses and

   C. The employee returns all excess reimbursements within a reasonable time

And,

Resolved, That the following methods will meet the "reasonable time" definition:

   A. An advance is made within 30 days of when an expense is paid or incurred

---

*Reprinted, with minor adaptation, by permission from *The Zondervan Church and Nonprofit Tax & Financial Guide: 2008 Edition* by Dan Busby, CPA (Grand Rapids: Zondervan, 2007), 77.

B. An expense is substantiated to the church within 60 days after the expense is paid or incurred or

C. An excess amount is returned to the church within 120 days after the expense is paid or incurred

And,

Resolved, That substantiation of business expenses will include business purpose, business relationship (including names of persons present), cost (itemized accounting), time, and place of any individual nonlodging expense of $75 or more and for all lodging expenses. Auto mileage reimbursed must be substantiated by a daily mileage log separating business and personal miles. The church will retain the original copies related to the expenses substantiated.

(Note: The above resolution includes the basic guidelines for an accountable expense reimbursement plan. If the church desires to place a dollar limit on reimbursements to be made under the plan on a staff member by staff member basis, simply add another paragraph such as:

And,

Resolved, That reimbursement of business expenses under this accountable reimbursement plan is limited to $_____ for 2009 for [name of staff member].)

Appendix 2

Agreement of Understanding

This agreement of understanding is between the following church and pastor:

Church: _____

Pastor: _____

This agreement, which presents the terms of the pastoral appointment by the conference stationing committee, is intended to reduce the possibility of wrong assumptions and misunderstandings on the part of the pastor or the parish. The goal is a healthy working relationship between pastor and congregation.

Starting Date

Employment will begin _____.

Salary

The annual salary is $_____ to be paid (circle one):

Weekly   Biweekly   Monthly

Social Security

State the amount of social security the church will pay the pastor this year. $_____

(Most churches consider half the cost of social security as part of the total pay package for their pastor. The amount is determined by combining the salary, housing, plus utilities, and multiplying by the government rate.)

If your pastor has opted out of the social security system, state how this benefit will be paid instead of a payment into the social security system.

_____

_____

Insurance

State the health insurance coverage the church provides for the pastor and family.

_____

State the disability insurance coverage.
_____

Housing

Will the church provide a parsonage or a housing allowance that will enable the pastor to rent or purchase a home?

Yes　　　　　　No

State the fair monthly rental value of the house, or the monthly housing allowance provided for the pastor.

Rental value: $_____ Monthly housing allowance: $_____

State any expectations or restrictions concerning the parsonage (if any).
_____
_____
_____

Utilities

What utilities will the church pay as part of the housing package?
_____

How are the utility bills paid?
___ Paid by the church treasurer
___ The pastor pays the utility bills and submits an expense voucher
___ Other (explain):_____

Vacation

State the number of weeks of vacation per year. _____

(Standard guidelines: two weeks for 1-5 years of service, three weeks for 6-10 years, four weeks for 11-20 years, five weeks for 21+ years)

How long does the pastor need to be at the church before receiving vacation time? _____

State any expectations of the pastor regarding vacation time.
_____

Continuing Education Budget

What is the annual continuing education amount budgeted for the pastor? $_____

Appendix 2

Moving Expenses

State the moving arrangements (rental truck, professional mover) and who is responsible for paying the moving expenses. _____

Travel Expenses for the Pastor

The church will pay _____ cents per mile for a maximum of _____ miles per year for ministry travel.

How often must the pastor turn in travel expenses to the church treasurer? _____

State any special arrangements regarding travel expenses. _____

Reimbursement Plan for Church Expenses

State the policy and procedure for the reimbursement of expenses incurred in the ministry (the cost of ministry should be paid by the church). Note: the IRS states that reimbursement of expenses cannot be deducted from salary.

What professional ministry expenses will the church cover?

___ Home entertainment   ___ Continuing education   ___ Book allowance
___ Work-related meals   ___ Ministerial luncheons, etc.   ___ Periodicals
___ Conference expenses
___ Professional dues   ___ Civic activities
___ Other (state) _____

Pension

(Define your church's pension plan. Churches that are part of a denomination should define their denomination's pension plan here.)

State the amount the church will contribute via a salary increase agreement to the 403*(b)* Plan. (The treasurer withholds the pastor's percentage via a salary reduction agreement each month.)
$_____

Review of Salary and Benefits
State when salary and benefits will be reviewed by the church's governing board.

_____

Special Understandings (schooling, working spouse, pets, etc.)

_____
_____
_____

Board Chairperson _____ Date _____
Pastor _____ Date _____
Date _____

Church of the United Brethren in Christ (www.ub.org/forchurches/PRCManual/Agreement_form.html). Used by permission.

Appendix 2

BUDGET INPUT LEDGER

	A	B	C	D	E
1	G/A General Ledger				
2					
3	Acct.				
4	No.	Account Name	Balance Forward	Current Activity	Balance
5	-----	------------------------------	------------------	------------------	------------------
6	1010	CASH IN BANK	($107.60)	($1,249.19)	($1,356.79)
7	1060	CASH ADVANCE - YOUTH PASTOR	$100.00	$0.00	$100.00
8	1070	CASH ADVANCE - VBS	$50.00	$0.00	$50.00
9	2030	FICA TAX	($13.78)	$0.21	($13.57)
10	2040	FEDERAL INCOME TAX	$30.00	$0.00	$30.00
11	2050	STATE INCOME TAX	$0.00	$0.00	$0.00
12	3010	GENERAL OPERATING FUND	$0.00	$0.00	$0.00
13	3011	CURRENT YEAR OPERATING FUND	($133.94)	$1,470.11	$1,336.17
14	3012	PRIOR YEAR'S DEFICIT (SURPLUS)	$0.00	$0.00	$0.00
15	3020	MISSION FUND	$0.00	$0.00	$0.00
16	3011	CURRENT YEAR MISSION FUND	$0.00	$0.00	$0.00
17	3012	PRIOR YEAR'S DEFICIT (SURPLUS)	$0.00	$0.00	$0.00
18	3030	EXPANSION FUND	$0.00	$0.00	$0.00
19	3011	CURRENT YEAR EXPANSION FUND	$0.00	$0.00	$0.00
20	3012	PRIOR YEAR'S DEFICIT (SURPLUS)	$0.00	$0.00	$0.00
21	3040	YOUTH PASTOR'S YOUTH FUND	$0.00	$0.00	$0.00
22	3050	WOMEN'S MINISTRIES	$0.00	$0.00	$0.00
23	3060	MEN'S MINISTRIES	$0.00	$0.00	$0.00
24	3070	ORGAN FUND	$0.00	$0.00	$0.00
25	3080	MORTGAGE RETIREMENT	$0.00	$0.00	$0.00
26	3090	NOT USED	$0.00	$0.00	$0.00
27	3097	GYM RESERVE	$0.00	$0.00	$0.00
28	3098	BUS PAINTING	$0.00	$0.00	$0.00
29	3100	NOT USED	$0.00	$0.00	$0.00
30	3110	NOT USED	$0.00	$0.00	$0.00
31	3120	TEENS	$0.00	$0.00	$0.00
32	3130	NOT USED	$0.00	$0.00	$0.00
33	3140	NOT USED	$0.00	$0.00	$0.00
34		INCOME ACCOUNTS			$0.00
35	4011	TITHES AND OFFERINGS	($45,979.23)	($9,504.40)	($55,483.63)
36	4022	EXPANSION FUND	($1,666.00)	($247.50)	($1,913.50)
37	4033	MISSION FUND	($3,961.51)	($775.00)	($4,736.51)
38	4043	OTHER MISSIONS	($173.98)	$0.00	($173.98)
39	4044	OTHER MISSIONS	$0.00	$0.00	$0.00
40	4052	RENTAL RECEIPTS	($11,000.00)	($1,500.00)	($12,500.00)
41	4053	GYMNASIUM RENTAL INCOME	$0.00	$0.00	$0.00
42		EXPENSE ACCOUNTS			$0.00
43	5011	DENOMINATIONAL BUDGET	$0.00	$0.00	$0.00
44	5012	NOT USED	$0.00	$0.00	$0.00
45	5021	P AND B (PENSIONS AND BENEFITS)	$0.00	$0.00	$0.00
46	5031	LOCAL DISTRICT EXPENSES	$0.00	$0.00	$0.00
47	5041	COLLEGE SUPPORT	$0.00	$0.00	$0.00
48	6011	FIRE AND LIABILITY INSURANCE	$2,208.52	$466.50	$2,675.02
49	6021	NOT USED	$0.00	$0.00	$0.00
50	6031	CHURCH VAN INSURANCE	$240.50	$0.00	$240.50
51	6041	NOT USED	$0.00	$0.00	$0.00
52	6051	UMBRELLA INSURANCE	$0.00	$0.00	$0.00
53	6061	HOMEOWNERS INSURANCE	$0.00	$0.00	$0.00
54	6101	ELECTRIC	$5,126.50	$1,706.79	$6,833.29
55	6111	TELEPHONE	$936.47	$174.13	$1,110.60
56	6121	WATER	$1,140.78	$358.28	$1,499.06
57	6131	GAS	$80.16	$40.58	$120.74
58	6141	TRASH	$489.75	$97.95	$587.70
59	6151	PARSONAGE ELECTRIC	$261.59	$0.00	$261.59
60	6161	PARSONAGE TELEPHONE	$0.00	$0.00	$0.00
61	6171	PARSONAGE WATER	$115.50	$0.00	$115.50
62	6181	PARSONAGE GAS	$83.19	$0.00	$83.19
63	6201	GENERAL MAINTENANCE	$2,337.99	$701.59	$3,039.58
64	6211	RENOVATION EXPENSE	$0.00	$0.00	$0.00
65	6221	CAPITAL EXPENSE OTHER	$0.00	$0.00	$0.00
66	6231	PARSONAGE MAINTENANCE	$0.00	$0.00	$0.00
67	6251	CHURCH VAN MAINTENANCE	$0.00	$0.00	$0.00

For the complete form, please see the CD.

THE CHURCH TREASURER'S MANUAL

MONTHLY BUDGET REPORT TO FINANCE COMMITTEE

	A	B	C	D
1				
2	OUR CHURCH NAME			
3	BUDGET REPORT FOR FINANCE COMMITTEE			
4		FOR MONTH OF:		
5				
6				
7			CURRENT YTD	ANNUAL
8			MONTH	BUDGET
9			-------	-------
10				
11				
12	TITHES AND OFFERINGS		(9,504)	($55,483.63) $ -
13	EXPANSION FUND		(248)	($1,913.50) $ -
14	MISSION FUND		(775)	($4,736.51) $ -
15				
16				
17	TOTAL INCOME		(10,527)	(62,134) $ -
18				
19	RENTAL RECEIPTS		(1,500)	($12,500.00)
20				
21				
22	DENOMINATIONAL BUDGETS			
23	GENERAL BUDGET		$0.00	$0.00 $ -
24	PENSIONS AND BENEFITS		$0.00	$0.00 $ -
25	LOCAL DISTRICT		$0.00	$0.00 $ -
26	COLLEGE SUPPORT		$0.00	$0.00 $ -
27				
28				
29	TOTAL BUDGETS		$0.00	$0.00 $ -
30				
31				
32	PROPERTY AND EQUIPMENT			
33	INSURANCE		467	2,916 $ -
34	UTILITIES		2,378	10,612 $ -
35	MAINTENANCE INCLUDING LAWN		702	3,223 $ -
36	VAN MAINTENANCE		0	0 $ -
37	EQUIPMENT		0	0 $ -
38	FEES AND ASSESSMENTS		100	143 $ -
39				
40				
41	TOTAL PROPERTY AND EQUIPMENT		3,646	16,893 $ -
42				
43	DEBT SERVICE		3,713	22,279 $ -
44				
45				
46	PERSONNEL			
47	PASTOR		2,545	11,419 $ -
48	MUSIC MINISTER		0	0 $ -
49	STAFF ASSOCIATE		0	8,054 $ -
50	YOUTH MINISTER		0	0 $ -
51	SECRETARY		0	0 $ -
52	PAYROLL TAXES		14	2,430 $ -
53	GIFTS TO STAFF		0	0 $ -
54	MEDICAL INSURANCE		1,507	4,902 $ -
55	NURSERY ATTENDANTS		177	1,346 $ -
56				
57				
58	TOTAL PERSONNEL		4,243	28,151 $ -
59				
60				
61	GENERAL EXPENSE			
62	SPECIAL EVENTS		134	878 $ -
63	ENTERTAINMENT		0	17 $ -
64	RETREATS/CONFERENCES		0	0 $ -
65	PASTOR CAR EXPENSE		0	0 $ -
66				
67				
68	TOTAL GENERAL EXPENSE		134	895 $ -
69				
70				
71	OPERATING EXPENSE			
72	OFFICE SUPPLY		29	372 $ -
73	POSTAGE		58	171 $ -
74	PRINTING		0	0 $ -
75	FLOWERS AND BENEVOLENCE		172	301 $ -
76				
77				
78	TOTAL OPERATING		259	843 $ -
79				
80				
81	OUTREACH			
82	VEHICLE EXPENSE		130	795 $ -
83	LITERATURE AND TAPE MINISTRY		0	144 $ -

For the complete form, please see the CD.

Appendix 2

ANNUAL BUDGET

	BUDGET
INCOME	
TITHES AND OFFERINGS	115,726
EXPANSION FUND	39,858
FAITH PROMISE	15,416
RENTAL INCOME	0
OTHER	
BUDGETS	
DENOMINATIONAL BUDGET	13,757
PENSIONS AND BENEFITS	3,668
LOCAL DISTRICT	10,547
COLLEGE SUPPORT	6,420
PROPERTY AND EQUIPMENT	
INSURANCE	6,000
UTILITIES	17,000
MAINTENANCE	5,200
RENTAL MAINTENANCE	0
BUS MAINTENANCE	0
EQUIPMENT	500
FEES AND ASSESSMENTS	100
DEBT SERVICE	4,699
PERSONNEL	
PASTOR	24,282
MUSIC MINISTER	0
STAFF ASSOCIATE	9,100
YOUTH DIRECTOR	0
CUSTODIAL AND LAWN	0
SECRETARY	4,290
PAYROLL TAXES	328
GIFTS TO STAFF	400
STATE COMP FUND	100
MEDICAL INSURANCE	5,442
NURSERY ATTENDANTS	1,500
GENERAL EXPENSE	
SPECIAL EVENTS	2,000
ENTERTAINMENT	300
RETREATS/CONFERENCES	0
PASTOR CAR EXPENSE	2,400
OPERATING EXPENSE	
OFFICE SUPPLIES	2,000
POSTAGE	1,000
LAWN MAINTENANCE	600
PRINTING	1,000
FLOWERS	500
OUTREACH	
VEHICLE EXPENSE	750
LITERATURE AND TAPE	750
PROMOTION	500
YOUTH MINISTRY	500
CHILDREN'S MINISTRY	1,000
SCOUTING	300
MUSIC	300
SUNDAY SCHOOL	2,000
VBS	250
MISSIONS	1,659
EXPANSION FUND	39,858

For the complete form, please see the CD.

THE CHURCH TREASURER'S MANUAL

ANNUAL BUDGET REPORT TO CHURCH

LOCAL INTERESTS:	
(A) Amount Raised for All Purposes	-74808
(1a) Buildings & Capital Expenditures	3183
(1b) Pastors Housing & Utility Allowance	2810
(2) Indebtedness on Property	19929
(3a) Pastor's Salary	11419
(3b) Pastor's Employee Benefits	5572
(4a) Associate Pastors' Salaries	8054
(4b) Associate Pastors' Employee Benefits	0
(5a) Local Church Expense	18755
(6) Local Department Expense	2608
(8) Other Benevolences (Local)	
(9) TOTAL LOCAL	-2478
DENOMINATIONAL DISTRICT INTERESTS:	
(10) District Budget	0
(11) District Home Missions	
(12) District Center	
(13) District Departmental Expense	
(14) Other Benevolences (District)	
(15) TOTAL DISTRICT	0
EDUCATION INTERESTS:	
(16) College Support	
(19) TOTAL EDUCATIONAL	0
GENERAL INTERESTS:	
(20) Denominational Budget	0
(22) Pensions and Benefits	0
(24) TOTAL GENERAL	0
(25) GRAND TOTAL	-2478

For the complete form, please see the CD.

Appendix 2

Sample Congregational Balance Sheet
Per Month/Year to Date

ASSETS	General Fund	Restricted Fund	Plant Fund	Endowment Fund	Total All Funds
Cash and Cash Equivalents	62,533	32,947	16,210	8,500	120,190
Accounts Receivable	1,768				1,768
Pledges Receivable			72,000		72,000
Other Current Assets	4,765				4,765
Land, Buildings, and Equipment			525,000		525,000
Investments	10,000	43,000		62,000	115,000
TOTAL ASSETS	79,066	75,947	613,210	70,500	838,723
LIABILITIES AND FUND BALANCE					
Accounts Payable	3,621			5,000	8,621
Payroll Withholding	524				524
Deferred Revenue	22,000				22,000
Current Portion Long-Term Debt			10,000		10,000
Long-Term Debt			150,000		150,000
TOTAL LIABILITIES	26,145	-	160,000	5,000	191,145
FUND BALANCES					
Unrestricted	52,921				52,921
Temporarily Restricted		75,947			75,947
Permanently Restricted				65,500	65,500
Net Investment in Plant			453,210		453,210
Total Fund Balances	52,921	75,947	453,210	65,500	647,578
TOTAL LIABILITIES & FUND BALANCES	79,066	75,945	613,210	70,500	838,723

Sample General Fund
Statement of Revenue and Expense
for the Month and Year-to-Date Ending (Current Month)

Support and Revenue	Month	YTD	Budget	Budget Remaining	% of Budget Rec'd/Spent
Contributions	26,417	247,123	305,000	57,877	81.02%
Interest Income	623	5,112	5,000	(112)	102.24%
Workshop/Events Income	214	600	1,000	400	60.00%
Total Support and Revenue	27,254	252,835	311,000	58,165	81.30%
Expenses (by Program)					
Worship	9,000	77,845	100,000	22,155	77.85%
Education	2,403	9,453	10,000	547	94.53%
Care/Fellowship	925	8,766	10,000	1,234	87.66%
Evangelism	1,613	8,453	10,000	1,547	84.53%
Resources	2,543	28,488	50,000	21,512	56.98%
Community Relief	800	2,475	3,000	525	82.50%
Youth	865	2,776	3,000	224	92.53%
Administration	10,325	111,457	125,000	13,543	89.17%
Total Expenses	28,474	249,713	311,000	61,287	80.29%
Excess of Support and Revenue Over Expenses	(1,220)	3,122	—	3,122	1.00%

Appendix 2

**Sample Statement of Revenue and Expenses
Per Month/Year to Date**

	General Fund	Restricted Funds	Plant Funds	Endowment Funds	Total All Funds
Support and Revenue					
Contributions	309,027	5,472	16,575		331,074
Interest Income	6,132	3,655	640	5,130	15,557
Workshops/Events Income	733				733
Bequests				10,000	10,000
Total Support and Revenue	315,892	9,127	17,215	15,130	357,364
Expenses (by Program)					
Worship	98,541	2,435		5,000	105,976
Education	10,205	750			10,955
Care/Fellowship	9,876	219			10,095
Evangelism	9,545				9,545
Resources	46,723				46,723
Community Relief	3,000	1,934			4,934
Youth	3,025				3,025
Administration	123,786		11,000		134,786
Total Expenses	304,701	5,338	11,000	5,000	326,039
Excess of Support and Revenue Over Expenses	11,191	3,789	6,215	10,130	31,325
Fund Balances at Beginning of Year	41,730	72,158	446,995	55,370	616,253
Fund Balances at End of Year	52,921	75,947	453,210	65,500	647,578

Sample Statement of Cash Flows
Per Month/Year to Date

Operating Cash Flows	General Fund	Restricted Funds	Plant Funds	Endowment Funds	Total All Funds
Excess Revenues (Expenses)	11,191	3,789	6,215	10,130	31,325
Adjustments:					
Depreciation	2,796				2,796
Change in Prepaid Expenses	(1,248)				(1,248)
Change in Accounts Payable	1,525				1,525
Change in Payroll Withholding	(78)				(78)
Change in Deferred Revenue	(6,525)				(6,525)
Net Operating Cash Flows	7,661	3,789	6,215	10,130	27,795
Financing Cash Flows					
Proceeds from Borrowings					-
Repayment of Debt			(25,000)		(25,000)
Net Financing Cash Flows			(25,000)		(25,000)
Investing Cash Flows					
Fixed Asset Sales (Purchases)	(5,755)				(5,755)
Purchase of Investments	(10,000)	(75,000)		(50,000)	(135,000)
Proceeds of Investments	-	60,000		47,000	107,000
Net Investing Cash Flows	(15,755)	(15,000)	-	(3,000)	(33,755)
Net Increase (Decrease) in Cash	(8,094)	(11,211)	(18,785)	7,130	(30,960)
Transfers	(10,000)		10,000		-
Cash and Cash Equivalents:					
Beginning Year	80,627	44,158	24,995	1,370	151,150
End of Year	62,533	32,947	16,210	8,500	120,190

Appendix 2

DATE	ITEM	TOTAL DEPOSIT	CHURCH	SUNDAY SCHOOL	YOUTH	MISSION

CASH RECEIPTS JOURNAL

For the complete form, please see the CD.

THE CHURCH TREASURER'S MANUAL

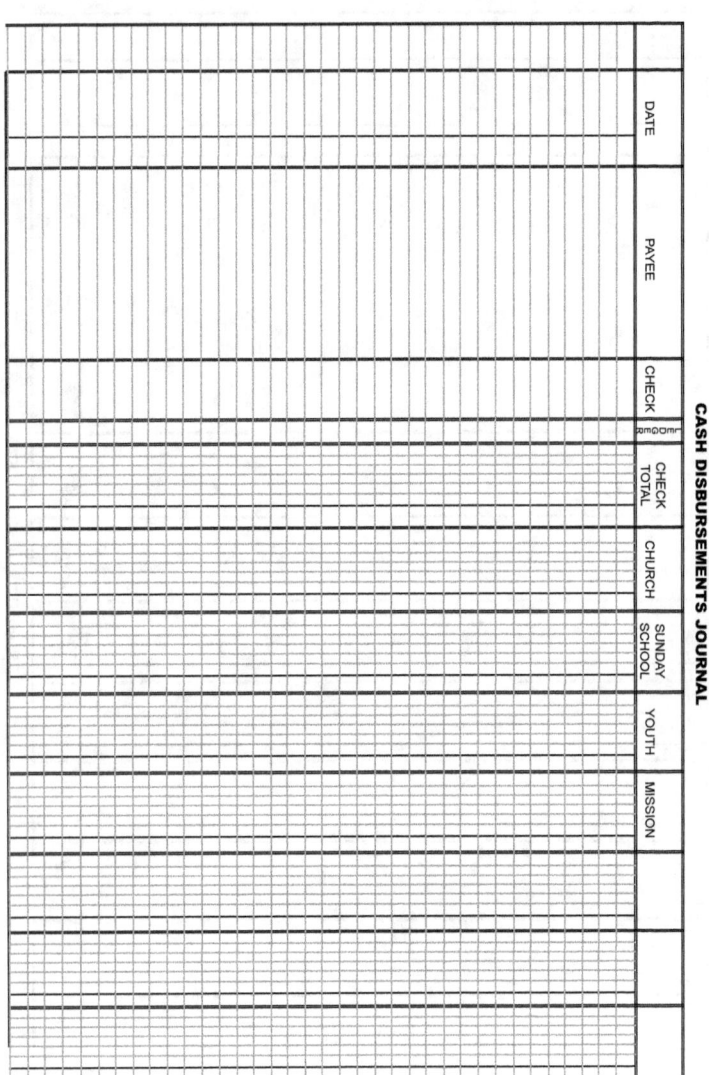

For the complete form, please see the CD.

Appendix 2

Account Name   **LEDGER**

DATE	ITEM	CHECK NO.	CURRENT	MONTH TO DATE	YEAR TO DATE

For the complete form, please see the CD.

www.ingramcontent.com/pod-product-compliance
Lightning Source LLC
Chambersburg PA
CBHW051402290426
44108CB00015B/2117